I hope you enjoy this book. You are the second biggest Cub fan I know besides me! I guess its true that "Misery enjoys company".

Lets have a Great Year this year, Dad!

All our Love
Aidan, Natalie
and
Son #2

CUBS

from **Tinker** ... *to* **Banks** ... *to* **Sandberg** ... *to* **TODAY**

by

JOE HOPPEL
and JOE DISTELHEIM

Sporting News BOOKS

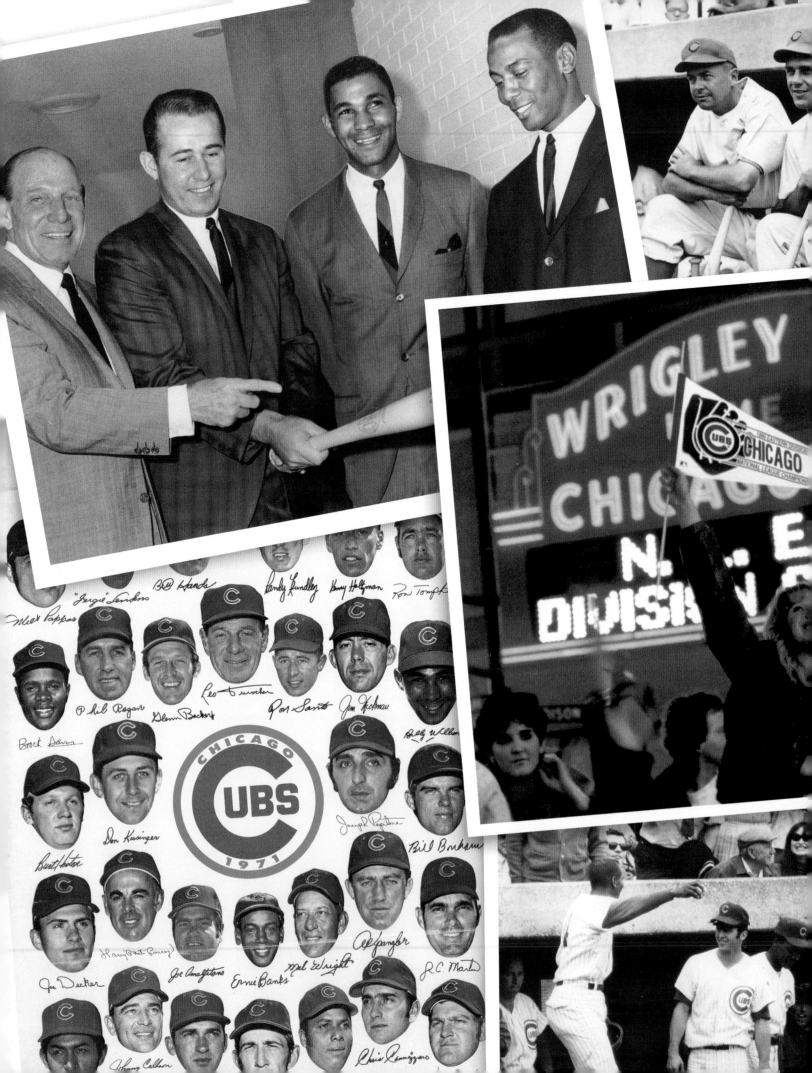

"Fergie Jenkins   Bill Hands   Randy Hundley   Kenny Holtzman   Ron Tompkins

Milt Pappas

Phil Regan   Glenn Beckert   Leo Durocher   Ron Santo   Jim Hickman

Brock Davis

Billy Williams

Don Kessinger   Joseph Pepitone

Burt Hooton   Bill Bonham

Harry (Peanuts) Lowrey   Al Spangler

Joe Decker   Joe Amalfitano   Ernie Banks   Mel Wright   J.C. Martin

Johnny Callison   Chris Cannizzaro

CHICAGO
CUBS
1971

WRIGLEY
CHICAGO
N.
DIVISION

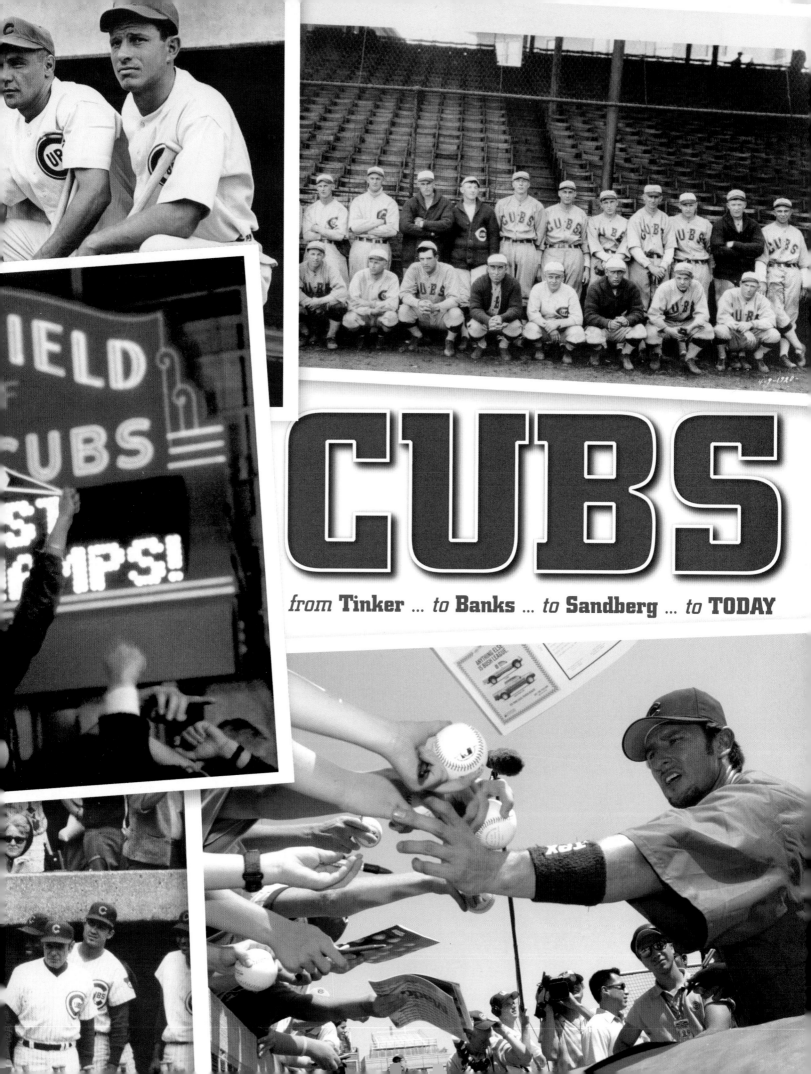

CUBS

from **Tinker** ... *to* **Banks** ... *to* **Sandberg** ... *to* **TODAY**

◆ **Joe Hoppel** is a Senior Editor for the Sporting News.

"I have been a Cubs fan since my boyhood days in Montana. I spent many a summer afternoon listening to the Cubs on Mutual's Game of the Day. (I could hear Pat Pieper in the background, announcing each batter.) I once wrote an offseason letter addressed simply "Frankie Baumholtz, Cleveland, Ohio"—and heard back within days. The 1955 Cubs—as opposed to, say, the '27 Yankees—are my favorite team of all time."

◆ **Joe Distelheim** is a free-lance writer living in Huntsville, Ala.

"I was a fan before the Cubs were cute, in the days they were just bad. I grew up on the South Side of Chicago, but my friends Jimmy Blasi and Arnie Skor were Cubs fans, and so was I. Jimmy's mother took us to Wrigley Field on Ladies Days if Jimmy hadn't been naughty. My favorite player was Randy Jackson; my mom stenciled his No. 2 on the back of a T-shirt."

Book design: Bill Wilson. **Cover design:** Bill Wilson. **Photo editor:** Michael McNamara.

Contributing writers: Sean Deveney, Shawn Reid. **Copy editors:** Dave Sloan, Dale Bye. **Page design & production:** Bill Wilson, Matt Kindt, Michael Behrens, Bob Parajon. **Research:** Steve Gietschier. **Photo research:** Jim Meier. **Prepress specialists:** Pamela Speh, Vern Kasal, Steve Romer.

PHOTO CREDITS

T = Top   B = Bottom   L = Left   R = Right   M = Middle

All photos TSN Archives unless otherwise noted.

Albert Dickson/TSN: 12-13, 17, 116BR, 172R, 173M, 218B

Jay Drowns/TSN: 5BR, 8, 10-11, 14, 16, 18-19, 22T, 27T, 34BR, 36TR, 38B, 39BL, 58 (2), 59, 97, 159TL, 222 (2), 223T

Charles Conlon/TSN Archives: 105, 136, 146TL, 190

Wide World Photos: 22-23, 23 (4), 25T, 25BL, 25MR, 26B, 28L, 29T, 29BL, 30 (3), 31B, 32-33, 36ML, 40L, 41R, 42B, 65, 73, 111, 117B, 119BR, 120BL, 128T, 131T, 140BR, 149BL, 150BM, 164, 167, 169 (2), 170, 171, 179 (2), 203, 216-217, 223B

National Baseball Hall of Fame and Library, Cooperstown, NY: 124MT, 143BR, 144L, 149BR, 166

AFLO/Allsport via Getty Images: 219T

Chicago Cubs/MLB Photos via Getty Images: 185

Louis Requena/MLB Photos via Getty Images: 158M

MLB Photos via Getty Images: 136BR

Library of Congress: 191

South Bend Tribune: 4TL

UPI/Corbis: 4-5T, 144, 201

Chris Bernacchi for TSN: 15

Jay Crihfield for TSN: 218T

Ronald L Mrowiec: 2-3

Peter Newcomb: 4-5M

Steve Woltman for TSN: 120M

ISBN: 0-89204-746-1   10 9 8 7 6 5 4 3 2 1

TINKER *to* EVERS *to* CHANCE

Joe Tinker, Johnny Evers and Frank Chance formed the first notable
double-play combination in major league history and were key components
of the only two Cubs teams to win World Series championships.

Contents

INNING 1

Looking Ahead

I t was a sun-splashed first
week of October in the
Wrigleyville section of
Chicago's North Side, with
the kind of crisp, clear days that
mark fall in the Midwest.
Chicagoans never take good weather for granted, and yet, something
was missing. This was perfect
weather for playoff baseball, and it
seemed that, somehow, there was
supposed to be playoff baseball in
town. Yet Wrigley Field was empty
in the early fall of 2004, and frustrated Cubs fans were left to bask
in the pleasantness outdoors, and
wonder what might have been.

With the Cubs coming off a
charmed 2003 season, one in which
the club won the Central Division
and was just five outs from the
team's first World Series appearance since 1945, few would have
predicted that the 2004 Cubs would
not be in the postseason. But, then,
few could have predicted the mis-
fortunes that would strike the
team. In the end, it was a wonder
that the Cubs had enough gump-
tion to fight through the messy
spate of injuries, fateful sneezes
and even a full-fledged hurricane,

**Kerry Wood (immediate left)
and Mark Prior each missed
two months of the 2004
season, but they figure to
show their old form in 2005.**

to finish 89-73 and remain in the hunt for the playoffs until collapsing in the final three series of the season.

Consider that the North Siders entered the season expecting to have the best young 1-2 pitching combination in the major leagues, with Mark Prior and Kerry Wood. But Prior, who won 18 games in 2003, suffered an inflamed Achilles' tendon in spring training and did not make his 2004 debut until June 4. Wood, a 14-game winner in 2003, had to sit two months with an injury to his triceps. The two struggled to overcome their injuries, and combined to go 14-13.

There was more. Slugger Sammy Sosa had to sit a month with back spasms caused when he sneezed too hard. Closer Joe Borowski tore his rotator cuff. Shortstop Alex Gonzalez suffered a broken wrist when he was hit by a pitch. So bad was the Cubs' luck that it was little wonder they were scheduled to be in Florida in September to face the Marlins when Hurricane Frances struck, raining out their series and forcing the Cubs into a demanding stretch of 26 games in 24 days. By the final week of the season, the

Cubs were still in position to earn a playoff spot, but, worn out, they had trouble scoring and protecting leads, and finally bowed out.

Cubs manager Dusty Baker called 2004—his 12th year as a major league manager—his toughest season. "But these guys busted their butts," Baker said after the season. "They gave it all they had."

Perhaps Cubs fans should take heart. Despite the debilitating injuries, Baker kept his club together, and showed why he is one of the best managers in the league. He gets the most out of players, and does not allow them to lean on excuses when things turn sour. Baker has managed the Cubs for just two years, but already has fans in Chicago believing the Cubs should be in the playoffs every year, an odd notion for a team that just finished back-to-back winning seasons for the first time since 1971-72. Cubs fans, in turn, showed their loyalty, as the team set an attendance record with more than 3 million fans.

Baker, a survivor of prostate cancer, is certainly looking forward to 2005. "I'm going to have fun," he said. "This is very, very, very important to me. Very important to me. When you've had cancer, you find different things that you realize aren't life threatening and you do what you can do. And next year will be different than this year."

Carlos Zambrano (left) appears on the verge of stardom for a Cubs team that at long last has a solid presence at third base in hard-hitting Aramis Ramirez.

Manager Dusty Baker has fans believing that the team should reach postseason play on a regular basis. A rotation that includes Wood, Prior, Zambrano and the ageless Greg Maddux (opposite page) gives Chicago a shot at supplanting St. Louis as the N.L. Central Division champion in '05.

As disappointing as 2004 might have been, there were enough positives to support Baker's optimism. One was the pitching of 23-year-old Carlos Zambrano, who kept the Cubs afloat during the injuries to Prior and Wood, and ranked fourth in the National League with a 2.75 ERA. He has steadily improved his control and demeanor each season in the big leagues, and possesses the talent of a staff ace. When the Cubs needed him most, Zambrano excelled, going 4-0 with a 1.01 ERA in September.

One of the highlights of the Cubs' summer came on August 7, when Greg Maddux bested the Giants, earning the 300th win of his career, making him just the 22nd pitcher to reach that milestone. With so much high-quality young pitching on board, the Cubs had the luxury of using Maddux fourth in the rotation. At age 38, he was sharp again in 2004, finishing with a 16-11 record and showing that he was one of the best free-agent signings of the offseason.

Two other relatively new acquisitions excelled on the offensive side. The Cubs have struggled to fill the third base hole since Ron Santo left the team after the 1973 season, but it appears that 26-year-old Aramis Ramirez, acquired during the 2003 season, is the long-term answer. Ramirez batted .318, drove in 103 runs and topped

Santo's single-season record for home runs by a Cubs third baseman with 36. Over his first six years in the majors, Ramirez struggled mightily defensively. After making 33 errors in 2003, he increased his concentration in '04 and committed just 10 errors.

Of course, fielders commit fewer errors when they're throwing to a Gold Glove first baseman, and the Cubs landed one in November 2003: Derrek Lee. Not only is Lee, who stands 6-5, a perfect fit at first base, but he is 29 and in the prime of his career at the plate. He belted 32 home runs and drove in 98 runs in '04 and is signed to stick around the

North Side for another two years.

Sosa, Ramirez, Lee and Moises Alou all hit at least 30 home runs, marking the first time in club history that four Cubs had reached that plateau. The Cubs showed they can be a dangerous team when it comes to slugging, leading the National League with a franchise-record 235 homers.

The Cubs should get even better. Corey Patterson is getting comfortable at the top of the lineup, where his speed (32 steals in '04) and power (24 home runs) can make him one of the best leadoff hitters in the league. He must work to cut down his strikeouts. Ramirez and

The return of shortstop Nomar Garciaparra, obtained at the 2004 trading deadline, is a big reason for renewed optimism on Chicago's North Side.

Lee seem capable of improving upon their already-impressive numbers. Zambrano may well emerge as an elite pitcher, and Prior and Wood figure to bounce back to their previous form. Plus, the ageless Maddux is on hand—and shortstop Nomar Garciaparra, the one-time Red Sox star, is coming back.

General manager Jim Hendry has a proven record of bolstering the club—his many moves during the 2003 season, his acquisitions of Lee and Maddux over the following off-season and his deal for Garciaparra at the 2004 trading deadline being proof positive. So, the Cubs are certain to enter the 2005 season fortified and ready to atone for '04.

The injuries, the seven losses in eight games as the season wound down, the rift between players and the TV booth and the negativity surrounding Sosa's early departure from Wrigley on the season's final day—all that will be ancient history. The Cubs will accentuate the positive. Even the expected departure of icon Sosa—he appeared headed to the Orioles in a trade—will be viewed as addition by subtraction, considering Sammy's growing discontentment and disruptive influence.

"I expect us to be better next year, much better," Baker said. "Defense, baserunning, bunting—we're going to tighten it all up big time."

Chances are, with Baker in command, Wrigley Field won't have such a lonely feel in future Octobers.

INNING 2

Cubdom

WE
are serfs in the Kingdom of Cub.

We are in thrall to the vines of the outfield, to the seventh-inning sing, to the pain of '69 and the shock of '84.

We are attached by heredity to Philibuck and Pafko, Sarge and the Hawk, Brickhouse and Caray, channel 9 and 720 on your radio dial.

We are descendants of those who watched the first Chicago National League ballclub, the one that essen-tially invented the league in the centennial year 1876, and then handily won its first pennant. We carry the flag of those who ringed fields on the south, west and north sides to watch Cap Anson and Three Finger Brown and

Spending a week at Randy Hundley's camp is a fantasy come true.

Swish Nicholson, league champions all. We are part of more than a century and a quarter of tradition, of Tinker to Evers to Chance, of Hack

to Hank to Banks.

We are of all ages, and we know no social boundaries.

We are those of the Greatest Generation, fast disappearing, who were around for the Homer in the Gloamin' and some of the greatest teams.

We share Cubdom with important people: the vice president and the late former president

and the junior senator from New York, and with the actors and coaches and other celebrities who sing "Take Me Out To The Ballgame," for better or worse. And we share Cubdom with the folks

Why, Charlie? Why did you pitch a clearly worn-out Borowy? We coulda been champs.

We share optimism, not self-delusion, with famous politicians, actor Bill Murray and folks of all ages and social backgrounds ... and we carry on for those who served in the kingdom but are gone now.

whose vacation of a lifetime is a Cubs Convention in wintertime Chicago cold or a week at Randy Hundley's fantasy camp in wintertime Arizona warmth.

We are those, into our Medicare years, who remember Gravel Gertie, baseball's most famous hot dog vendor, and who still wonder why manager Charlie Grimm started Hank Borowy on short rest in Game 7 in '45.

We share Cubdom with the late cartoonist Jeff MacNelly:

Shoe (wearing Cubs cap): A good Cubs fan accepts defeat and disappointment in the belief that tomorrow will be a better day. Do you know what that's called, Skyler?

Skyler: Self-delusion.

Shoe: Optimism is the word I was looking for.

We are those, now thinking about retirement, who waited for the Andy Frain ushers to stop paying attention, in the days when the Cubs really did play two, then sneaked down into the always-available box seats. There, up close, you could see Handsome Ransom Jackson at third base next to Roy Smalley, and Frankie Baumholtz playing the outfield among the mastodons, Hank Sauer and Ralph Kiner.

We share Cubdom with those who have transported the blue circle and the red C all over the world, to places like Puerto Vallarta in Mexico, which is where you find Mickey's No Name Cafe, "Unofficial Home Chicago Cubs."

We are those whose mind's picture of the Friendly Confines always shows a bright daytime scene, who always want to know if the wind's blowing in off the lake or blowing fly balls into the seats, who know to bring a jacket even in June.

We share Cubdom with the cap-wearing, kid-bringing, glove-carrying crowds that hurry off the el at the Addison stop, and with those who can score space on the rooftops, and with those who pack the beer bistros around the park. We inhabit this land of ours with Bleacher Bums who wear no shirts and with generals of industry who wear suits and cell phones. And we share Cubdom with those who come no closer to the team than WGN on cable.

We are those, in the midst of our careers now, who scattered far from Chicago and picked up the pre-cable, pre-Internet voices of Vince Lloyd and Lou Boudreau after dark amidst the static on the radio. Sometimes, you did better in your car; maybe that's how you heard the late-night Hendley-Koufax no-hit duel in Los Angeles.

We picked up the pre-cable, pre-Internet voice of Vince Lloyd (left). And, hey, we heard Jack Brickhouse's "Hey, hey" not nearly enough times.

We share Cubdom with those who come no closer to the team than WGN on cable.

Attending the wintertime Cubs Convention is the vacation of a lifetime. It's a lot like going to Wrigley Field—the place is packed and fans are focusing their attention on Dusty Baker and Ryne Sandberg.

We share Cubdom with political writer and occasional Cubs commentator George Will, who uses the same skybox-price words to describe the infield fly rule and the McCain-Feingold Act, and with political writer and occasional Cubs commentator David Broder, who does not.

We are those who went from ecstasy to gloom in 1969 with Fergie and Santo and the New York Stinkin' Mets. And we are those who went from I-94 Series anticipation to a winter's depression in the course of one week in 1984—the Padres, for Ryne's sake!

A red state-kind-of-guy, George Will favors blue (and Ron and Fergie) when it comes to baseball.

How many Cubs fans lived long and otherwise fulfilling lives without seeing their team

We share Cubdom with the people we spot with Cubs caps on the beach and with Cubs stickers on their California bumpers and with Cubs shirts in the stands at Turner Field in Atlanta (our super station can beat yours!). We have nothing else in common with the bearers, but we are extended family, serfs performing the duties of our station in life.

We are those who, through good fortune of birth, were spared these old agonies and first felt the lash in October 2003, in an eighth inning that will hurt as long as anyone can remember the names of the fan who turned one maybe-out into none and the shortstop who turned a sure two into none.

We share Cubdom with the generations who have heard "I don't care who wins as long as it's the Cubs," and "Hey, hey," and "Holy Cow!" We have common points of reference: "The beer refreshing," Quinlan and Boudreau cracking up as they touted ladies' slips for sale at Goldblatt's. We share images: "Beautiful Wrigley Field," the manual scoreboard, bullpens right there

in the open down the base lines. We know that 8/8/88 was the date of the first (rained-out) night game, and that Waveland is the avenue behind the left field bleachers. I say Brock. You say Broglio. And we remember together the awful trade.

We are those who carry on for those who served but are gone now, all the potential-springs-eternal fans who saw new hope in Novikoff and Brinkopf, Baker and Banks, Drott and Drabowsky, the hope we see today in Wood and Prior. We who have bowed before Andy and Billy and Sammy are the successors to

Any team can have a bad century, but few teams can boast of an icon like Ernie Banks, Mr. Cub.

win four of seven in the last week of the baseball year?

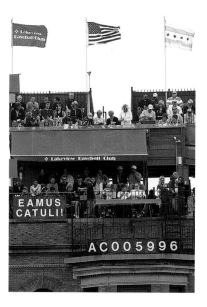

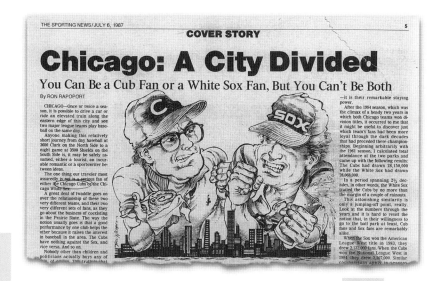

THE SPORTING NEWS/JULY 6, 1987

COVER STORY

Chicago: A City Divided
You Can Be a Cub Fan or a White Sox Fan, But You Can't Be Both

By RON RAPOPORT

CHICAGO—Once or twice a season, it is possible to drive a car or ride an elevated train along the eastern edge of this city and see two major league teams play baseball on the same day.

Anyone making this relatively short journey from day baseball at 3600 Clark on the North Side to a night game at 3500 Shields on the South Side is, it may be safely assumed, either a tourist, an incurable romantic or a sportswriter between ideas.

The one thing our traveler most assuredly is not is a serious fan of either the Chicago Cubs or the Chicago White Sox.

A great deal of twaddle goes on over the relationship of these two very different teams, and their two very different sets of fans, as they go about the business of coexisting in the Prairie State. The way the notion usually goes is that a good performance by one club helps the other because it raises the interest in baseball in the area. The Cubs have nothing against the Sox, and vice versa. And so on.

Nobody other than children and politicians actually buys any of this, of course. The truth is that

—it is their remarkable staying power.

After the 1984 season, which was the climax of a heady two years in which both Chicago teams won division titles, it occurred to me that it might be useful to discover just which team's fans had been more loyal through the dark decades that had preceded these championships. Beginning arbitrarily with the 1961 season, I calculated total attendance at the two parks and came up with the following results: The Cubs had drawn 28,150,000 while the White Sox had drawn 28,068,000.

In a period spanning 2½ decades, in other words, the White Sox trailed the Cubs by no more than the margin of a couple of rainouts.

This astonishing similarity is only a jumping-off point, really. Look at the numbers through the years and it is hard to resist the notion that, in their willingness to go to the ball park at least, Cub fans and Sox fans are remarkably alike.

When the Sox won the American League West title in 1983, they drew 2,132,000 fans. When the Cubs won the National League West in 1984, they drew 2,107,000. Similar comparisons apply in seasons

We are not about to abandon our heritage, and we'll never envy fans who attach themselves to that corporate entity in the Bronx. Pulling for the White Sox is never an option, but a loud GO CUBS! (EAMUS CATULI!) always is.

the many who revered Hack Miller and Hack Wilson and Hack, Stan. How many millions of unrequited Cubs fans, people who worked hard and gave to charity, were good to their spouses and children, were honest and upright ... how many lived long and otherwise fulfilling lives without seeing their team win four of seven in the last week of the baseball year?

We are those who can recite the whole litany of dropped fly balls and botched grounders and horrid personnel decisions.

We've all heard the line: Any team can have a bad century.

Why do you put yourself through this, they ask, they who do not share our lot in life. Why do you care so much when the object of your affection keeps spurning you? They don't say it in so many words, but they imply that we should abandon our heritage, that we should abdicate.

People, please understand. We do

not envy Yankees fans. Who roots for Microsoft to make another billion? We are not like fans of the Diamondbacks or the Marlins, those World Series arrivistes of the Sunbelt. Rooting for such a team is drinking instant coffee.

The White Sox, clearly, are not an

option.

We cringe at the phrase "long suffering," which lazy language attaches to "Cubs fans" the way it attaches "lovable" to "losers." We

More than a half-century ago, we bowed before Andy Pafko in the same way those who came before us revered Hack Wilson and other favorites.

We share Cubdom with the Bleacher Bums, many of whom visit watering holes on game day and some of whom were the subject of a 1970s stage play (above).

know the real emphasis in that expression is on "long." We who are of a certain age were Cubs fans before the Cubs were cute. We are not those who change team alliances like so many Dave Kingmans. If the job takes us to Houston, we are sure as grass not going to start pulling for some team that plays on synthetic fiber in an airplane hangar with cup holders.

The enterprise of our estate has never been stuffy and old money, nor is it upstart nouveau riche. It's everyday, solid, Middle American, like, well, the Wrigley Co. Chew on that.

We don't know five World Series championships in a row, or a baker's dozen division titles and counting. But that only makes us appreciate smaller successes all the more. How joyful were those six months of 1984, right through the third day of October and a two-games-to-none lead in the championship series? How wonderful was the unexpected Boys-of-Zimmer 1989 season? Yes, Mark McGwire outhomered Our Sammy in '98, but who got into the postseason? And 2003, in the division playoff, how about flicking the Braves away like so much lint?

We who are of a certain age were Cubs fans before the Cubs were cute.

We will not waver in our loyalty, or in our passion. We will persevere. We trust the lords of the manor, trust they are with us in the struggle.

We believe that the current general manager is a fine judge of baseball flesh, and will employ workers who are strong of mind and body, powerful of arm, fleet of foot, and of good character. Men named Gallagher and Matthews and Holland and Green (oh, so close!) and Lynch couldn't do it, but this time we are on the right path. We have faith.

We pay homage to our guys in creative ways, and we proudly pass down our Cubdom to future generations.

We know—not hope, know—that the manager we have now is finally the man to show our troops the way to ultimate victory, as no one has since the Peerless Leader, Frank Chance, in ought-eight. Jolly Cholly couldn't, or the Fordham Flash, or Marse Joe, not the entire faculty of the college of coaches, not the roaring Leo or the ranting Lee, not all

We share Cubdom with Bryant Gumbel: 'Being a Chicago Cubs fan is like being in limbo, with paradise always a day away.'

the guys named Jim. But this is the time.

We share Cubdom with Bryant Gumbel:

"Being a Chicago Cubs fan is like being in limbo, with paradise always a day away."

We take the long view of the unpleasantries of 2004, the season of

promise unfulfilled. We know that, despite it all, we were just two Sammy sneezes and two simple saves from a second postseason in a row.

Our day will come, though we worry that it won't. And—admit it— we worry a little that it will. In the most secret parts of our minds we wonder what will happen to us, to

our very being, if the Cubs really do win it all in our lifetimes. Then how will we feel about them? How will we feel about ourselves? What would the dog do if it did catch the school bus? And if Sisyphus had gotten the stone to the top? Then what?

If disappointment is the coin of the realm, we know no other. If anticipation of a better year next year is the air we breathe, it is as vital as oxygen.

Long live the kingdom.

Being a Cubs fan is for the young and the young at heart. Sure, the object of our attention often spurns us—but not always, as the 2003 N.L. Central Division championship and ensuing Division Series victory proved.

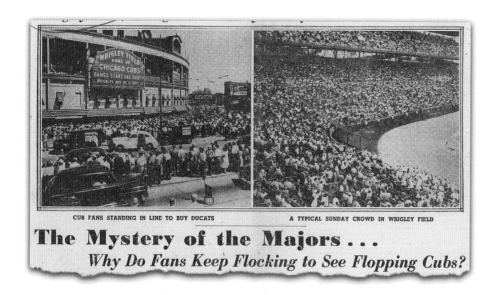

CUB FANS STANDING IN LINE TO BUY DUCATS   A TYPICAL SUNDAY CROWD IN WRIGLEY FIELD

The Mystery of the Majors . . .
Why Do Fans Keep Flocking to See Flopping Cubs?

The Sporting News' question about the loyalty of Cubs fans—a query made in 1948—didn't need an answer then and doesn't require one now if you're a serf in the Kingdom of Cub.

INNING 3 Wrigley

Field

33

"The windows and roofs of flat buildings across the way from the park were crowded with spectators," the *Chicago Tribune* reported. "The surface and elevated trains leading to the north side were overhanging with people in the early afternoon. ..."

No surprise there. After all, it was opening day at the ballpark at Clark and Addison streets.

More from the *Tribune*:

"The weather was far from suited to the occasion ... A chilling wind was coming off the lake and one needed winter furs to be comfortable. Regardless of conditions, the fans turned out in hordes."

No surprise there, either.

Only thing is, what now seems so quintessentially "game day" at the baseball palace was not typical at all when those passages were written. They appeared in the April 24, 1914, edition of the *Tribune*—the day after the first-ever game was played at the gleaming new park, home of the Chicago Whales of the fledgling Federal League.

That the Whales and their upstart league went belly up after two seasons was a huge disappointment to investors and players who hoped to win acceptance for baseball's third major league. But if the Federal League's demise—and the Whales' existence along with it— marked the end of the line for a grandiose baseball scheme, it also made possible the beginning of one of the great romances in sports history, a love affair between Joe fan, his team and a ballyard.

It all came about when Charlie Weeghman, owner of the Whales and the park in which the team played, turned around and purchased Chicago's National League franchise—the highly successful Cubs—and immediately moved his new charges from their not-so-venerable West Side Grounds to the greensward bounded by Clark, Addison, Waveland and Sheffield. On April 20, 1916, the Cubs played their first game at Weeghman

Tucked into the Wrigleyville neighborhood of Chicago and home of the Cubs beginning in 1916, Wrigley Field draws a short-sleeve or even shirtless crowd to its bleacher sections in the heat of summertime.

Sitting in front of Wrigley's landmark scoreboard makes it difficult to keep an eye on inning-by-inning scores from out of town, but bleacherites are a content and boisterous lot—and known to swill a beverage or two.

Broadcaster Harry Caray, honored with a statue outside Wrigley, turned the seventh-inning stretch into a singalong. Since Caray's death in 1998, selecting a guest singer has become something of a circus.

Park—later to be called Cubs Park and later yet Wrigley Field, both after William Wrigley Jr. took control of the team—and defeated the Reds, 7-6, on Vic Saier's 11th-inning single.

The interior of the baseball plant had a vastly different look in 1916 than it does now—one deck, no towering scoreboard, no vines. Yet, standing in the vicinity of where The Cubby Bear now sits, a fan gazing over at Weeghman's showcase would have seen an outer shell that looked surprisingly similar to today's Wrigley Field.

When Cincinnati's Johnny Beall whacked a home run onto the porch of a building on Sheffield Avenue that day, the ball did not magically wind up back on Wrigley's bluegrass. There was no seventh-inning singalong, no Andy Frain ushers to show you to your seat. Yet, when you left the park and walked along Waveland Avenue toward Clark Street, there stood a little firehouse—the one that still serves the neighborhood today as Engine 78. And when you left the park and walked along Addison Street toward Sheffield Avenue, there, rumbling overhead, was the elevated train. It still rumbles.

All the while, on your postgame stroll in 1916, you might have

WGN's Jack Quinlan (middle) and Lou Boudreau (right) called a 1964 game from a fresh perspective—the bleachers.

reflected on the velvet tones—the unmistakable tones, anyway—of Pat Pieper, through whose bullhorn you heard the starting lineups (Max Flack ... Heinie Zimmerman ... Saier ... Claude Hendrix). Fifty-eight years later, you still would have heard Pieper introducing players (Rick Monday ... Jerry Morales ... Billy Williams ... Bill Bonham).

There is something to be said—something reassuring—about such continuity.

For nearly two decades, though, the Cubs' new home was really not unlike other major league parks. Everyone played day baseball, on grass and in mostly no-frills stadiums. Then came night baseball, electronic scoreboards, artificial grass and amusement-park-like

One gate may be closed (below), but by game time the upper deck and the rest of the Cubs' home at Clark and Addison streets will be filled or close to capacity.

stadium monstrosities in suburban settings where, it seemed, baseball was almost an afterthought.

For Philip K. Wrigley, who succeeded his father as Cubs owner, baseball was somewhat of an afterthought, too. Wrigley never cared terribly much for the game, but he had great respect for his franchise's standing in the community—and for anyone who spent money on his products, be it chewing gum or baseball.

That respect for the paying public was evident in the product that he and his father had assembled at Wrigley Field, the Cubs winning four pennants from 1929 through 1938 and boasting some of the game's best and brightest stars. His bond with the fans also became

Fans gather on rooftops (right), in the street to catch home run balls and at such intersections as Waveland and Sheffield (below) for pregame and postgame conviviality. Many die-hards ride the elevated train (opposite page, bottom left) to Wrigley, where vendors await at the main entrance.

evident within the infrastructure and friendly confines of the steel, concrete and brick facility.

Just five years into his ownership of the Cubs and a decade after the park had been double-decked, Wrigley embarked in 1937 upon a "beautification plan." There were skeptics aplenty at the start, but once new, expanded and comfortable bleachers were added—and a mammoth scoreboard erected—there was a sense that something was a-happening here. Then, when Wrigley instructed an aspiring baseball man within his front office—a gent named Bill Veeck—to deck the walls with

vines of ivy, well, OK, this was pretty neat stuff.

Sure, Wrigley's entrepreneurial mind was at work—such a setting couldn't help but lure more fans to what was now "beautiful Wrigley Field"—but one sportswriting critic grudgingly acknowledged that P.K.'s

No. 1 objective in this project was to achieve "scenic distinction."

Wrigley wasn't done. He soon ordered the installation of wider chairs in the box-seat and grandstand sections, despite the reduced seating capacity it would create. And seats in the outer reaches of the park, down the lines, were turned toward home plate to afford fans a better view of the action.

Whatever the vantage point, what a place to watch a ballgame: The sun shining brightly on the lush grass; the ivy, the filled-to-capacity bleachers and the rooftop gatherings across Waveland and

Sheffield serving as a backdrop to what unfolds on the field; pennants and flags blowing briskly and gloriously atop the scoreboard, the upper deck and the foul poles; the nice-as-your-grandmother ushers, smiling and helpful and sometimes even doting; the proximity to the field, making it seem as if you could reach out and snatch a cap off a rival player's head; players signing autographs over the little brick wall that runs from dugout to

dugout; Wayne Messmer singing the national anthem; the palpable excitement as everyone awaits the first pitch; the hand-operated, massive-but-quaint scoreboard keeping fans informed on how, say, the hated Cardinals are doing (man, St. Louis has been out for a long time in the fifth inning); the sev-

Wrigley's confines weren't so friendly in 2000 when a fan near the bullpen stole a cap from a Dodgers player.

enth-inning stretch, a time to look toward the WGN booth, wonder who's going to mangle "Take Me Out to the Ball Game" on this day ... and join in the fun.

P.K. Wrigley thought you could watch the goings-on quite nicely without the aid of artificial illumination. The installation of lights would take a toll aesthetically, even if night games might prove a significant revenue enhancer for a team operating in a 40,000-seat

Never accused of being fair-weather fans, Cubs faithful take delight in the beauty of the ivy-covered walls and the merriment provided by a band that tours the stands. Not everyone was thrilled with the installation of lights in 1988, but fans and the park itself have survived.

ballpark; more important, he reasoned, night ball would be an intrusion upon Wrigleyville, whose graceful homes and close-knit neighborhoods would be subject to traffic congestion, parking hassles, lawn trampling, potential rowdyism and various other indignities that seem to worsen once the sun goes down.

The Tribune Company, which

In 1955, Cubs fans in a designated area could hear Jack Brickhouse's account of the game on overhead speakers. Things looked much the same then as they do now (poles included) at the park, which had some structural problems in 2004.

purchased the Cubs from the Wrigley family in 1981, didn't quite see it that way. Downplaying any inconveniences nighttime baseball might inflict and ignoring any impact on the park's charm factor, it instead argued that the addition of lights was an economic necessity if Wrigley Field were to continue as home of the Cubs. Seven years later, night baseball was being contested at Clark and Addison—a development that clearly angered the baseball gods. In the fourth inning of the first scheduled night game—August 8, 1988, vs. the Phillies—the heavens unleashed a torrential downpour. Game called. "The first time I tried it with the lights on, it was pretty much a washout, too," David Letterman cracked.

The Cubs and Mets got the knack of it the next evening—Letterman, we don't know—and Chicago came out a 6-4 winner at Wrigley. Now, the nighttime schedule goes from 22 games in 2004 to 25 in 2005. And to 28 or 30 in 2006. Wrigley Field survives.

Wrigley is not everyone's favorite ballpark. Fenway Park, another true original, admittedly is a worthy choice, and Yankee Stadium, a once-done-over baseball cathedral, has to rank high on any list—even if its makeover three decades ago gave it an essentially new feel. Despite our clear-cut vote, there are dissenters in other precincts, too.

Some fans, after seeing the glitz of new parks, think Wrigley is just too old (something about crumbling underpinnings), and that it

A souvenir ball would have been nice, but in '04 this young fan had to settle for a chunk of concrete that fell from the upper deck.

lacks all, most or even some of the modern conveniences. Many players gripe about the cramped clubhouse conditions. More than a few observers from afar see the park as a bandbox where wind-aided homers skew statistics and outcomes. (Don't those folks realize that it's 355 and 353 feet down the foul lines to the fences in left and right field? Don't they know how often the wind blows IN?) Even Babe Ruth, the man who hit or quite possibly did not hit a called-shot homer here, was moved to say, "I'd play for half my salary if I could hit in this dump all the time." What a kidder, that Ruth, who, subjected to untoward taunting from Cubs fans during the 1932 World Series, taunted right back.

Greg Maddux wasn't kidding, though, when in 2004 he talked to a

reporter for the *Chicago Tribune* about his feelings for the Cubs, their fans and their ballpark after the conclusion of his back-home-again season: "It's a privilege to play here, it really is. This place makes baseball special."

For Joe fan, the emotional connection is just as sincere, deep, lasting. It's a privilege to go there, it really is.

There are stops along the way, to meet friends at Murphy's Bleachers or The Cubby Bear, to gather 'round the Harry Caray statue, to duck into the souvenir shops. But there's nothing like fun at the ol' ballpark itself, particularly this ol' ballpark—the one whose huge, red sign above the main entrance at Clark and Addison tells you that you're exactly where you want to be.

If the 1908 Cubs' mascot didn't strike fear in the hearts of opponents, the team itself did. Frank Chance's club won its third consecutive pennant and second straight World Series championship. A member of the National League since the N.L.'s inception in 1876, the Chicago franchise has won 16 pennants overall.

INNING 4

44

Champions

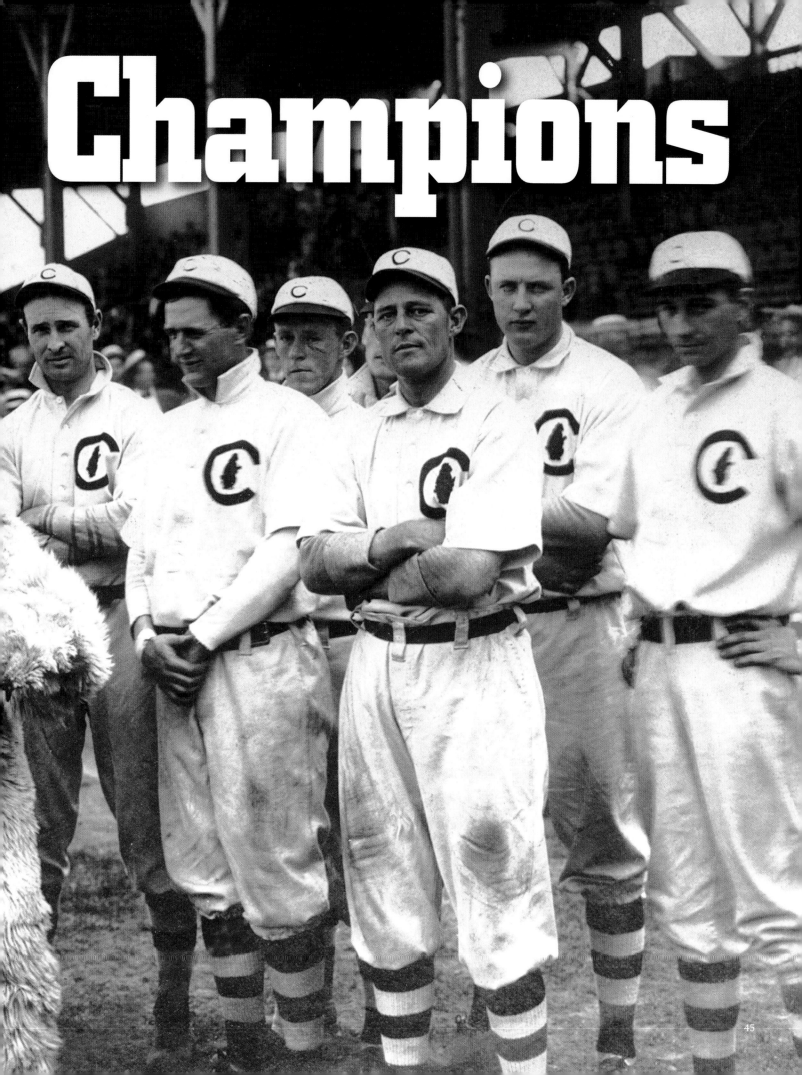

The Cubs' cup is half full: They have won 16 pennants, three division championships and one postseason wild-card berth. Starting in 1984, they went to the postseason four times in 20 years after going 0-for-38.

The Cubs' cup is half empty: They haven't won a World Series since 1908. Their total of Series crowns—two in the 100 major league seasons that have been capped by a fall classic—is matched by the Florida Marlins, who began play in 1993.

History shows that the Cubs have had their glorious moments, notably three eras in which there was no better team in the National League. Unfortunately, that's ancient history. In the past six-plus decades, through 2004, success has consisted of one wartime pennant (and a subsequent World Series defeat), those three division titles (followed twice by first-round eliminations, once by a heartbreaker in the League Championship Series) and the one wild-card spot (an adventure that ended in a three-game Braves sweep).

At first, in fact, the Chicago team was the equivalent of the latter-day New York Yankees in its dominance. Return with us now to those thrilling days of yesteryear. ...

Exactly two months before the Indians knocked George Custer out of the game, Al Spalding shut out Louisville and the Chicago National League ballclub was on the way to its first championship in the league's first year, 1876. With manager Spalding pitching almost every day, the "White Stockings" played

nearly .800 ball, taking the title by six games over a 66-game season. Chicago's Ross Barnes led the league in hitting, but the fulcrum was third baseman Adrian Anson, who soon would become first baseman-manager "Cap" Anson and the leading figure in the team's first run of success.

By 1880, Spalding had retired as a player but had teamed with Anson to assemble the squad that

Outfielder George Gore swung a long, menacing bat for Chicago's powerful 1880 National League champions, leading the N.L. in hitting with a .360 average. Gore also played for the franchise's pennant-winning 1881, 1882, 1885 and 1886 teams. Second baseman Fred Pfeffer was a defensive standout who joined the team in 1883 and became a key member of the "Stonewall Infield."

play out the decade. That team played a postseason series, a raucous traveling show against St. Louis of the American Association that ended in a tie. There would be one more title. The **1886** team won by 2½ games, over Detroit—in the longest season yet, 124 games—but lost the semiofficial road show to St. Louis. The Anson Age would run almost to the end of the century, but its pennant-winning days were done.

Frank Chance arrived on the Chicago roster the year after Anson left. No one could have guessed that this 20-year-old substitute catcher-outfielder on the 1898 team would outshine Cap's accomplishments as a team leader.

The Cubs had good-but-not-great teams under Frank Selee in the early years of the 20th century, the first of the N.L.-A.L. structure that still exists. They put together the famous Tinker-Evers-Chance combination in the infield and a strong pitching staff led by Ed Reulbach and Three Finger Brown. But Selee was increasingly feeling the effects of tuberculosis, and in midseason 1905, he resigned. The players chose Chance—a strong hitter with both bat and fists—as their new manager.

The results were immediate. The Cubs were too far behind to get

Johnny Evers hated the rival Giants "honestly and furiously."

would dominate the league for years. Shortstop Tom Burns, outfielder Mike (later "King") Kelly joined incumbent third baseman Ned Williamson and outfielder George Gore, giving Chicago by far the most productive offense in the league. Gore led the league in hitting, new pitchers Larry Corcoran and Fred Goldsmith won 64 games between them, and the team won the pennant by 15 games. Its .798 winning percentage is the best in National-American League history.

The next two years were more of the same. In **1881**, the same cast won by nine games; in **1882**, the margin was three. After two off years, a retooled pitching staff led by John Clarkson's 53 victories gave Chicago the **1885** pennant in a race with the team that would become its chief rival for many years, the New York Giants. By that time, the White Stockings had added Fred Pfeffer at second base, joining Anson, Burns and Williamson in the "Stonewall Infield" that would

Manager Frank Chance (immediate right) was master of all that he oversaw.

back in the race that year, but improved their record markedly in the last two months. The next year, **1906**, they were in full throttle. With the additions of 20-game-winner Jack Pfiester and third baseman Harry Steinfeldt, they compiled what is still the best winning percentage (.763) of baseball's modern era. Those Cubs—and so they were now called in most quarters—won 116 games and lost just 36. They led the league in batting, fielding and pitching, and finished 20 games ahead of the second-place Giants.

After going 116-36, Wildfire Schulte and Co. weren't so hot in the '06 World Series.

All the more amazing, then, that they lost the World Series, four games to two, to their Chicago rivals, the "Hitless Wonders" White Sox. The sixth-game clincher started badly for the Cubs: A policemen kicked outfielder Wildfire Schulte as he went into the crowd circling South Side Park, unsuccessfully chasing a first-inning fly ball. "You're a fine bunch of stiffs," Chance told his team after the Series loss.

The next two seasons turned out to be the most productive in team history: two pennants, two World Series titles. With the same regulars in place, the **1907** team won 107 games. Pittsburgh finished second, but the rivalry with the Giants still was the hottest. Police fired guns into the air to scatter a mob after the Cubs beat New York one day at the Polo Grounds. Pitching carried the team, which had no .300 hitters. Orval Overall won 23

games, and four others won 15 or more. After the first game of the World Series ended in a tie, suspended by darkness, the Cubs won four straight over the Tigers, holding Detroit star Ty Cobb to a .200 average.

The **1908** race, unlike the past two, was no runaway. Indeed, it was one of the most exciting in history. That was the year of the Fred Merkle blunder, the year of the Reulbach doubleheader shutouts, the year the Cubs won the pennant in what amounted to a one-game playoff (officially, it was a makeup game) against, of all teams, New York at the Polo Grounds under near-mob conditions. (Johnny Evers: "If you didn't honestly and furiously hate the Giants, you weren't a real Cub.") The World Series was easier. Overall won twice, as did Brown, whose 29 victories that season are the most for a Cub since the mound was moved to 60 feet, 6 inches from home plate. Chicago over Detroit in five.

The Cubs won five more games in 1909 than in '08, but Pittsburgh was even better, winning 110 to the Cubs' 104. The same Chicago victory total in **1910** was plenty good enough. With the addition of sensation rookie pitcher "King" Cole (20-4, 1.80 earned-run average), the Cubs ran away from the Giants by

Before the 1910 Series, the Cubs' Chance (left), Three Finger Brown (third from left), Jimmy Sheckard (second from right) and Jimmy Archer enjoyed a light moment with the Philadelphia Athletics' Eddie Plank and Harry Davis.

13 games, giving Chance's champs their fourth pennant in five years. The World Series, however, belonged to Connie Mack's Philadelphia Athletics. The Cubs didn't hit, field or pitch very well; they lost the first three games, rallied to win the fourth, and succumbed at home in the fifth.

Many major league players entered the service in the final year of World War I, **1918**, and the regular-season schedule that year wrapped up on Labor Day. The Cubs, under manager Fred Mitchell, won the pennant in a watered-down league. This team had not a single holdover from the pennant-winning club of eight years previous. Rookie shortstop Charlie Hollocher was the hitting star, batting .316. Even in the shortened year (the Cubs played 129 games), lefthanders Hippo Vaughn and Lefty Tyler won 22 and 19 games, respectively, by far the best Cubs season ever for lefthanded pitching. In the World Series, the pre-curse Red Sox beat the pre-curse Cubs in six games, with Boston pitcher Babe Ruth winning two games and allowing just two runs.

By **1929**, the Cubs under Joe McCarthy had put together a fearsome foursome of Hack Wilson (.345), Kiki Cuyler

Rogers Hornsby put up huge numbers for the Cubs in 1929, a year in which both the team and the stock market ultimately crashed.

(.360), Riggs Stephenson (.362) and newly acquired Rogers Hornsby (.380), all of whom drove in more than 100 runs. The Cubs won the pennant over Pittsburgh by 10½ games. Unfortunately, the team with the famous offense came to an infamous end in the Series. This was the October of the Game 4 collapse (as opposed to future October unravelings in Game 5 and Game 6). With an 8-0 lead, Chicago was on the way to squaring the Series with the Athletics at two games apiece. As fly balls bounced around outfielders Wilson and Stephenson, the A's scored 10 runs in the seventh inning. In Game 5, the Cubs blew a 2-0 lead in the ninth and lost, 3-2. Little more than two weeks later, the stock market crashed, too.

It was a quite different team that won the Cubs' next pennant just three years later. McCarthy was gone, and nearly 100 games into the **1932** season, so was his successor, Hornsby, replaced by first baseman Charlie Grimm. Wilson was a Dodger, and Chicago had a new shortstop-second base combination, Billy Jurges and Billy Herman. Catcher Gabby Hartnett, who had missed most of the '29 pennant-winning season with a sore arm, was an offensive and defensive force. The character of the team shifted from offense (the first-place Cubs out-homered

only three teams) to pitching. Lon Warneke, who had previously won just two games as a Cub, was 22-6 with a 2.37 ERA. Late in the season, the team won 14 games in a row, and Chicago won the pennant by four games over Pittsburgh. This was the World Series of the Babe Ruth "called shot" legend; more than that, this was a Yankees team that had six future Hall of Famers in the field and three in the pitching rotation. It was four games and out.

The Cubs kept fielding winning teams, and broke to the top again in

1935. Like a long-running Broadway show, they'd replaced much of the cast while staying good. Since '32, youngsters Phil Cavarretta and Stan Hack had moved into the corner infield spots and speedy switch hitter Augie Galan, .325 hitter Frank Demaree and slugging Chuck Klein made up Grimm's outfield. Big Bill Lee joined Warneke as a 20-game winner. After being third, 9½ games behind the Giants, at the All-Star break, the Cubs got themselves back into the race. Then, in September, came a miraculous streak: They won 21 games in a row. The next-to-last victory in the streak clinched the pennant. Reported the Associated Press: "Rising to the crest of baseball greatness and crushing even the mighty Dizzy Dean with a devastating 15-hit barrage, the sensational men of Grimm capped their almost unbelievable drive today by battering the Cardinals 6 to 2 for their 20th straight victory and the National League pennant."

No luck in the World Series again, though. Despite splitting the first two games in Detroit, despite an injury to Tigers star Hank Greenberg, the Cubs fell in six.

By 1938, former player/manager Jolly Cholly Grimm was exclusively a bench manager. When the team got off to a mediocre start, it turned again to the player ranks. This time, it chose the catcher. Manager Hartnett did fine: A .556 team played .620 ball under him for the second half of the season, with 22-game winner Lee pitching four of his nine shutouts in September. And Hartnett hit the most famous home

Lon Warneke won a total of 42 games for the Cubs' N.L. champs of 1932 and 1935, and catcher Gabby Hartnett (above) was an offensive and defensive force. Chuck Klein (left), new to the club in 1934, hit 21 home runs in '35.

The pitching staff for the Cubs' last World Series team, the 1945 club, was headed by (from left, above) Claude Passeau, Hank Wyse, Paul Derringer, Hank Borowy and Ray Prim; the infield was manned primarily by (from left, above right) Phil Cavarretta, Don Johnson, Lenny Merullo and Stan Hack; the outfield corps was made up of (from left, at right) Harry "Peanuts" Lowrey, Frank Secory, Bill Nicholson, Andy Pafko and Ed Sauer; and the No. 1 catching job was held by Mickey Livingston.

run in Cubs history, the one in the Wrigley Field autumn twilight that beat Pittsburgh and finally put the Cubs ahead of the Pirates in the standings. With another great finish—21-5 in September—the Cubs won the pennant by two games.

The less said about the Series that year, the better: The Cubs scored nine runs in a four-game Yankees sweep, and Hartnett, the jovial catcher, became Hartnett, the screaming manager, on the train ride home from New York.

Charlie Grimm was back as manager by **1945**, and too old to go to war. Cardinals star Stan Musial wasn't, and found himself in the Navy, a fact that helped the Cubs edge St. Louis by three games. The heralded midseason acquisition of

Hank Borowy (11-2) certainly helped, but the Cubs had four other starters who won more games, led by Hank Wyse's 22 victories. Cavarretta had an MVP season, hitting .355. The Cubs again were not Messrs. October. Borowy and Claude Passeau shut out the Tigers in two of the first three games of the Series, but Grimm went to his new ace one too many times. Borowy, worn down after two Series starts and one relief appearance (a four-inning stint in Game 6 after he had

started Game 5), was Grimm's choice to pitch Game 7. The Tigers had a five-run lead before the Cubs came to bat. Ballgame.

Let us pause here, and reflect. With the N.L. title in hand and the boys coming home from the war, the Cubs—long before the arrival of that division stuff or wild cards—had won 16 pennants in 70 seasons. Hardly a record to suggest that for the next 59 years, through 2004, the Cubs would not add a single league championship.

Manager Charlie Grimm (below) got shutouts from Borowy (right) and Passeau in Games 1 and 3 of the '45 World Series but wound up going to his new ace, ex-Yankee Borowy, one too many times.

CHICAGO CUBS

Top Row- Lotshaw, Trainer; Wyse, P; Warneke, P; Starr, P; Erickson, P; Hanyzewski, P;
 Roy Johnson, Coach; Signer, P; Sauer, OF; Hughes, IF; Schuster, IF; Stock, Coach.
Middle Row- Passeau, P; Livingston, C; Derringer, P; Rice, C; Williams, C; Prim, P;
 Chipman, P; Vandenberg, P; Secory, OF; Becker, IF; Smith,Coach.
Bottom Row- Hack, IF; Don Johnson, IF; Lowrey, OF; Cavaretta, IF; Pafko, OF; Grimm, Manager;
 Nicholson, OF; Gillespie, C; Merullo, IF; Borowy, P; Jimmie Chalikis, Bat Boy.

When a special camp (left) was conducted in Lake Worth, Fla., in January 1946 for returning servicemen in the Cubs' organization, the big club was the defending National League champion. No one has referred to the Cubs in such a heady manner since.

Ryne Sandberg, one of many imports from Philadelphia, was merely sensational for the 1984 N.L. East-winning Cubs.

The Cubs did have the N.L.'s best team in **1984**; few people more than an hour's drive from the original SeaWorld would disagree. Dallas Green had come from the Phillies to be general manager and soon imported a bunch of their players. Philly veterans Gary Matthews, Keith Moreland, Bob Dernier and Larry Bowa graced the regular lineup, as did sensational Ryne Sandberg, who'd never had the chance to shine there. Green revived an ailing pitching staff by adding Dennis Eckersley and Rick Sutcliffe during the season. The Cubs, managed by former Kansas City chief Jim Frey, knocked out the Mets in September, finished 6½ games ahead of them, and looked forward to the World Series against the Tigers, the class of baseball that year.

And then came the San Diego Padres. The Cubs had them down two games to none. No team had ever won the NLCS from that position. But an ordinary pitcher, Ed Whitson, stopped the Cubs in

A crucial addition in '84, Rick Sutcliffe also notched 16 wins for the surprising 1989 division winners.

Game 3, smug Steve Garvey hit a dramatic homer off relief ace Lee Smith to beat them in Game 4, and first baseman Leon Durham's error in the finale became a classic "Oh, no" moment in Cubs history. Padres win.

In **1989**, the Cubs fielded a team of which little was expected. When the weather got warm, the Boys of Zimmer began to simmer, playing .624 ball over their last 85 games. Don Zimmer's team took advantage of fine rookie years from outfielders Jerome Walton and Dwight Smith, and got solid pitching from Greg Maddux, Sutcliffe and Mike Bielecki, a pickup from Pittsburgh. The Cubs got by with erratic but usually effective-in-the-end relief pitching from Mitch Williams. They also had solid '84 holdovers Sandberg and Scott Sanderson, and a knack for come-from-behind victories.

After winning the East Division by six games, Chicago drew San Francisco in a playoff series that was marked by otherworldly hitting by the two first basemen, the Cubs' Mark Grace (.647) and the Giants' Will Clark (.650), and by disappointing pitching on both sides. Maddux and ex-Cub Rick Reuschel both got rocked, but Reuschel came back to win the clincher, Game 5. (The NLCS was now best-of-seven.)

For a year that ended in the disappointment of a first-round playoff sweep, **1998** was a gloriously

Kerry Wood (above) and Sammy Sosa (opposite page) helped secure a 1998 wild-card berth for Chicago, which five years later got great pitching from young Mark Prior and nearly reached the World Series.

memorable one for Chicago. Coming off a season in which they'd lost their first 14 games and 94 altogether, the Cubs started fast, reveled in rookie Kerry Wood's 20-strikeout game in May, and sat back to watch Sammy Sosa duel the Cardinals' Mark McGwire. Before the season was over, Sosa had hit 66 home runs, more than anyone in pre-'98 major league history—but four fewer than McGwire.

Baseball's greatest home run race almost obscured a superb run for the postseason. The Cubs of Jim Riggleman, fielding a roster of mostly journeymen except for Sosa

and Wood and old pro Grace, won 90 games. They took the wild-card spot in a playoff win over the Giants, a 5-3 game filled with gripping moments. After that, though, the Braves made instant wood chips out of the Cubs' bats, and it was three and done in the postseason.

And then there was **2003**, still too recent to contemplate dispassionately. You can read elsewhere about the disastrous last 11 innings of that season. Here, as we conclude a

chronicle of Cubs success, are the good parts:

Under new manager Dusty Baker, the Cubs improved by 21 wins and won the Central Division in an exciting last weekend. New general manager Jim Hendry plucked the Pirates for several key parts down the stretch, notably veteran leadoff man Kenny Lofton and third baseman of the future Aramis Ramirez. Marvelous young pitchers Mark Prior and Carlos Zambrano

joined Wood in a starting corps that was the envy of all baseball. Marginal relief pitcher Joe Borowski became an ace closer at age 32. Sosa, despite being beaned and banished (for a corked bat), hit at least 40 homers for the sixth consecutive year. And the Cubs won a postseason series for the first time since 1908, whipping the Braves in five games.

Only thing left to say: Wait 'til next year.

INNING 5
The All-Tim

e Team

● **Manager** *1905-12; player, 1898-1912*

Frank Chance

The man who rode the Cubs to their only two World Series championships would make today's toughest managers seem as tender as scenes from *Field of Dreams*. It was either John L. Sullivan or Jim Corbett, both former heavyweight champs, who first called him "the greatest amateur brawler in the world." Frank Chance, the "Peerless Leader," did have boxing experience, and was noted for enforcing discipline on his troops with a solid punch to the gut. He also was known as "Husk," another tribute to his physique and toughness.

He put up with no nonsense. His message to his players was, "You do things my way or you meet me after the game." He would fine his men for shaking hands with opposing players. When fans in Brooklyn threw bottles onto the field, he threw them back.

Chance was a playing manager, of course. He started as a catcher, moved to the outfield with the arrival of Johnny Kling, then eased in at first base in 1902, the year Joe Tinker and Johnny Evers arrived to form the famous infield. When manager Frank Selee was forced to leave the club because of illness in late July of 1905, he asked the players to vote on his successor. At 27, Chance, who'd had a strong hand in putting together the team, was elected.

The Cubs played improved ball under him that

year, then ran off three pennants in a row and two straight World Series titles (1907, 1908). Pitching, defense and smart play characterized his teams. In 1906, his first full season as manager, the Cubs won 116 games. That still stands as the National League record, even though teams for years have been playing 162 games, not the 154-game schedule of Chance's era.

'The greatest amateur brawler in the world.'

In a five-year stretch beginning with that record-setting season, Chance's Cubs averaged 106 victories, had a winning percentage of .693 and won four pennants.

Frequent beanings—he habitually crowded the plate—sent Chance to surgery after the 1912 season to remove blood clots from his brain. Recuperating in the hospital, he demanded a four-year contract. Owner Charles Murphy fired him.

Chance has the highest winning percentage (.664) of any of the 55 men who have managed the Cubs. But it's as a player that he was elected to the Hall of Fame. His lifetime batting average was just under .300, and he was good defensively. And although he was a 190-pounder, he's the Cubs' all-time leader in steals with 404, including 67 in one season (1903).

CUBS CAREER	
Won: 768	
Lost: 389	
Winning percentage: .664	
Pennants: 4	
World Series titles: 2	

● **Catcher** *1922-40; manager, 1938-40*

Gabby
Hartnett

CUBS CAREER
Games: 1,926
Runs: 847
Hits: 1,867
Home runs: 231
Runs batted in: 1,153
Batting average: .297
Stolen bases: 28

Charles Leo Hartnett is the catcher on anybody's all-time Cubs team. Why?

Well, after a century and a quarter, he leads everyone who has ever been a Cubs catcher in nearly every offensive category. He had an awesome arm and an aversion to errors. And he hit the most celebrated home run in team history. Any questions?

"The Homer in the Gloamin'" is the most-told Gabby Hartnett story. It was September 28, 1938. The Cubs were trailing the first-place Pirates by a half game and facing Pittsburgh in Wrigley Field. The score was tied, darkness was falling, and it was clear that the Cubs' turn at bat in the ninth would be the last of the day. If the game ended in a tie, it would be played again as part of a doubleheader the next day, and Pittsburgh had the better-rested pitching staff.

Player-manager Hartnett homered into the left field bleachers with two out, on an 0-2 pitch. "The mob started to gather around Gabby before he had reached first base," the *Chicago Tribune* reported. "By the time he had rounded second, he couldn't have been recognized in the mass of Cub players, frenzied fans and excited ushers but for

that red face, which shone out even in the gray shadows."

Having seized first place, the Cubs stayed there and won their fourth pennant in 10 seasons. They'd win just one more league title in the 20th century.

Gabby Hartnett was equally a hero to common folk and a pal to celebrities. Hartnett knew Al Capone, whose Prohibition liquor business was among his lesser sins. Chastised by the baseball commissioner for having his picture taken with Capone at the ballpark, Hartnett said, "I go to his place of business. Why shouldn't he come to mine?"

Hartnett was a good-natured player who would talk to batters from his own place of business, behind the plate. His nickname, though, was an ironic one, pinned on him by a sportswriter who found the young Hartnett unusually reticent.

In addition to The Homer, Hartnett was part of other famous moments: He was catcher for Carl Hubbell's five consecutive strikeouts of Hall of Famers-to-be in the 1934 All-Star Game, and was behind the plate when Babe Ruth hit his supposed "called" home run in the 1932 World Series.

After a century and a quarter, he leads everyone who has ever been a Cubs catcher in nearly every offensive category.

First base *1876-97*

Adrian "Cap" Anson

Yes, it was a long time ago, but few have had as much impact on the game and the Cubs as the larger-than-life figure that was Cap Anson.

As an influential baseball man of his time, he led the player defection that created a viable National League. As a player, he swung a powerful and effective bat and helped Chicago to the new league's first pennant. As a manager, he led his team to 1,282 victories and five league titles.

Anson stood more than 6 feet tall, weighing well over 200 pounds. His manner made him appear ever bigger: He was loud, arrogant, theatrical. He did not keep his opinions to himself; famously, he adamantly and publicly opposed letting blacks play professional baseball.

his career, thus the nickname "Cap," for "captain." He's credited with inventing the base coach and the pitching rotation, with being among the first to take his team to spring training, with using what would become today's hit-and-run play. He was tough on his players, and got away with it even in an era in which it was easy for them to walk away, and he was intimidating to umpires, who worked alone in those days.

His Hall of Fame plaque calls him 'the greatest hitter and greatest National League player-manager of (the) 19th century.'

CUBS CAREER	
Games:	2,276
Runs:	1,719
Hits:	3,041
Home runs:	96
Runs batted in:	1,715
Batting average:	.334
Stolen bases:	247

He moved to Chicago with Albert Spalding and others to give the city an immediately successful team, then called the White Stockings, in the new league. As a first baseman, he anchored the "Stonewall Infield" that stayed together for seven years in the 1880s. Generally, he hit cleanup, rarely striking out, hitting .300 or better 19 times and winning four batting titles. He was the first player with 3,000 hits.

Anson became manager early in

His Hall of Fame plaque calls him the "greatest hitter and greatest National League player-manager of (the) 19th century." Unfortunately, he left the team in a bitter feud with Spalding, lost money in business and struggled for the rest of his life, trying barnstorming and vaudeville.

Anson died in 1922, when Babe Ruth and other glamorous stars were bringing baseball new popularity. His Chicago funeral attracted a massive crowd. His request for his headstone: "Here lies a man who batted .300."

● **Second base** *1982-94, 1996-97*

Ryne Sandberg

CUBS CAREER

Games: 2,151

Runs: 1,316

Hits: 2,385

Home runs: 282

Runs batted in: 1,061

Batting average: .285

Stolen bases: 344

He hit, ran, fielded and powered his way into 10 All-Star Game starts and into near sainthood among Cubs fans.

Here's Harry Caray in the 10th inning, Cubs vs. St. Louis, Wrigley Field, June 23, 1984: "There's a drive, way back—it might be out of here! It is! He did it again! Oh, the game is tied! Unbelievable! ... Listen to this crowd! ... Holy cow! What would the odds be if I told you that twice Sandberg would hit home runs off Bruce Sutter? ..."

It was one of the most memorable wins in Cubs history, 12-11, in 11 innings on national television. It also was one of the most memorable individual efforts in baseball history: Ryne Sandberg hit game-tying homers in the ninth and 10th innings against the best relief pitcher in baseball. He wound up with five hits, seven runs batted in, and this accolade from Cardinals manager Whitey Herzog: "Ryne Sandberg is the best baseball player I've ever seen."

The man who was a supposed throw-in when the Phillies and Cubs swapped shortstops in 1982 hit, ran, fielded and powered his way into 10 All-Star Game starts and into near sainthood among Cubs fans. That he was a man of sterling character as well—quiet, non-controversial, meticulously prepared for games—just added to the legend,

which now includes a place in the Hall of Fame.

Sandberg was a 20th-round draft choice as an 18-year-old. He was 22 as the Cubs' third baseman in his rookie year, then moved to the position at which he would run up numbers superior to most Cooperstown inductees who played at that spot. His 277 home runs as a second baseman set a record (since broken by Jeff Kent). He won N.L. MVP honors in '84, once led the league in homers and had back-to-back 100-RBI seasons. And he won nine consecutive Gold Gloves, setting a major league record that still stands by playing 123 consecutive games without an error at second.

In 1993, Sandberg signed a four-year, $28 million contract, making him, at that time, the highest-paid baseball player in history. And then he quit. Mired in a slump and with the Cubs in last place, Sandberg said on June 13, 1994: "I'm certainly not the type of person who can ask the Cubs and Cubs fans to pay my salary when I'm not happy with my mental approach and performance."

After a year and a half away from the game, Sandberg returned to the Cubs for two more seasons. His skills diminished, by Sandberg standards, he retired for good at age 38.

● Third base *1960-73; radio analyst, 1990-present*

He could do everything in a baseball uniform except run fast, but it's legs you think of when you hear Ron Santo's name these days.

The legs that leaped to click his heels when the Cubs won, starting when all was going right for the '69 team. The legs he has lost to diabetes—the disease he played through with astounding durability his whole career.

Santo was an eight-time All-Star Game participant, a home run-hitting cleanup hitter, a strong-fielding third baseman who won five Gold Glove awards, a slugger who reeled off a 28-game hitting streak.

He was an emotional player whose fiery personality contrasted to the quiet Ernie Banks and Billy Williams, the other big Cubs stars of the era—and at times got him in trouble. His spats with manager Leo Durocher got nasty and public, and his loudly expressed ire at outfielder Don Young's sloppy play in a 1969 game against the Mets made him temporarily a bad guy to Wrigley Field fans.

Starting when he'd just turned 20, Santo played more than 2,100 games at third base, more than anyone else ever has for the Cubs. It became an annual endeavor to count the number of players the Cubs have tried at third base since he left. Over an 11-year span, he averaged 159 games a season. In Cubs history, he's top-half dozen in games played, at-bats, home runs, total bases, extra-base hits and runs batted in.

His Type 1 diabetes was diagnosed when he was 18. Some around the Cubs knew, but he kept the condition from the public for many years. He didn't want to use it as an excuse when he didn't play well, he said. So he took his daily insulin shots in private, and discreetly kept chocolate bars in the dugout, and had days like the two in May 1966 when he won consecutive games with extra-inning homers, or the one in 1969, when his three-run homer won a Ken Holtzman no-hitter, 3-0.

He went public with his disease in 1971, just before the Cubs threw a "Ron Santo Day," with gifts going not to him, but to benefit diabetes research.

Santo's No. 10 is one of three numbers the Cubs have retired—along with those of longtime teammates Banks and Williams. He has been part of the radio voice of the Cubs since 1990—a voice that still clicks when the Cubs win.

CUBS CAREER

Games: 2,126
Runs: 1,109
Hits: 2,171
Home runs: 337
Runs batted in: 1,290
Batting average: .279
Stolen bases: 35

Ron Santo

He played through a disease with astounding durability.

● **Shortstop** *1953-71; coach, 1967-73*

Ernie Banks

This is not overstating the case: The day in September 1953 when Ernie Banks appeared for the first time in a major league lineup was the birthday of the America's Team Cubs we know today.

To understand, you have to know that the bare facts—512 home runs, fielding records, MVP awards, All-Star selections, first Cubs number retired—don't even get you to first base, the position at which Banks finished his first-ballot Hall of Fame career. His importance is far beyond that.

For a half century now, he has been the most purely popular face of a team that has inspired a national following far out of proportion to its achievement. Credit his ridiculously sunny personality—"Let's play two!" Note his longevity and loyalty.

But there's more than

image here. Ernie Banks changed a team and changed baseball in ways still apparent. He changed the expectation that Cubs have white skin, and the expectation that middle infielders hit singles.

On September 17, 1953, he became the first black to play for the Cubs. Banks was 22. He had never played what is defined within the game as "Organized Baseball." The Cubs got him from the Kansas City Monarchs, the renowned Negro leagues franchise.

He reported to the Cubs the same day as Gene Baker, another former Monarch the Cubs had been grooming as a shortstop in their farm system. General manager Wid Matthews said he added Banks to the roster because "we needed a roommate for Baker."

The ideal shortstops of the 21st century are the 200-hit Nomars and the

57-homer A-Rods. The prototypical shortstops half a century ago were handy fielders who hit—or more often didn't—at the bottom of the order.

Banks hit 47 home runs in his first MVP year of 1958, a major league record for the position. The next year, he hit 45 homers and became the first National League player deemed most valuable two years in a row. How good was he in '59? His 143 RBIs were the league's best in 22 years. For good measure, he made just 12 errors in more than 800 chances, setting a record for fielding percentage by a shortstop.

The Cubs finished tied for fifth both of those MVP years. It was an apt microcosm for Banks' 19-year Cub career: individual excellence, team frustration. On his retirement in 1972, Ernie Banks said, "I always wanted to bring a pennant to Wrigley Field. It's the one disappointment in my life."

CUBS CAREER
Games: 2,528
Runs: 1,305
Hits: 2,583
Home runs: 512
Runs batted in: 1,636
Batting average: .274
Stolen bases: 50

Ernie Banks changed a team and changed baseball in ways still apparent.

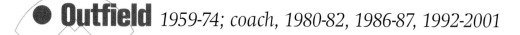

● Outfield *1959-74; coach, 1980-82, 1986-87, 1992-2001*

Williams Billy

One day in 1960, Rogers Hornsby, a Cubs minor league batting instructor and one of baseball's all-time best hitters, got in touch with the parent team while visiting Class AAA affiliate Houston.

"Suggest you bring up Williams," he said. "Best hitter on team." A Cubs official replied: "He's better than anyone else down there, huh?" Hornsby: "He's better than anyone up there."

Billy Williams, who'd had a brief Cubs trial in 1959, got another look in 1960, then set Cubs records for homers and RBIs by a rookie (25, 86) in 1961 and was named N.L. Rookie of the Year.

From that point on, there was unanimity about Williams: He could hit. He would play every day. And he'd go about his business quietly.

In 1970, after Williams set what was then the National League record for consecutive games played, columnist Jim Murray wrote: "Williams comes from a long line of people who show up for work every day. Like all such, Billy was as quiet, steady, dependable as a railroad watch. Every employer should have one. They give him a watch at the end of 50 years, and the boss' son, who inherited the business, notes at the banquet, 'He never missed a day at the lathe in his life.'"

Another writer guessed that Williams "wouldn't say 'rah! rah!' if Phil Wrigley promised him a $10,000 bonus for each 'rah!'"

But his bat did not escape notice—not the bat that hit 20 or more home runs in 13 consecutive seasons and produced three 200-hit seasons. Former teammate Lou Brock called him "the best hitter I ever saw."

Like his Hall of Fame contemporaries Willie Mays, Willie McCovey and Hank Aaron, he hailed from the Mobile area in south Alabama, but Williams was from a tiny town and didn't have the reputation of the others. He got no bonus when he signed with the Cubs—and wound up among the team's all-time leaders in practically every offensive category. Only Cap Anson and Banks have had more hits in a Cubs uniform. Only Sammy Sosa and Banks have hit more homers. Only Anson, Banks and Sosa have driven in more runs.

Toward the end of his playing career, Williams was traded to the A's. Despite Oakland's record of success—the A's ruled baseball from 1972 through 1974—he missed playing in a World Series there, too.

He eventually returned to the Cubs, serving as a coach and in the front office in several administrations. Quietly.

'Williams comes from a long line of people who show up for work every day. Billy was as quiet, steady, dependable as a railroad watch.'

● **Outfield** *1926-31*

Wilson Hack

'He was built along the lines of a beer keg, and not unfamiliar with its contents.'

Lewis "Hack" Wilson just might have had the greatest offensive season in major league history.

Wilson, who had played unspectacularly for the Giants from 1923-25, spent just six years with the Cubs. The fifth of those was 1930, when the first lively-ball era peaked. Everybody hit. Wilson hit more than everybody. He drove in 191 runs (research later changed the longtime record-book entry of 190); no one has reached 180 in more than 65 years. He hit 56 home runs, setting a National League record that stood for 68 years. He batted .356.

And he did all that with a stubby body he abused with the alcohol that would kill him at age 48 less than two decades later.

As a fictional character, Wilson would be a caricature, a home run hitter of prodigious talent, a power-ful brawler with a sixth-grade education, a drinker of mammoth repute in a day when ballplayers were expected to be carousers. In the words of longtime sportswriter Shirley Povich, who saw Wilson play, "He was built along the lines of a beer keg, and not unfamiliar with its contents."

Bill Veeck Jr., decades later, told of the time Wilson went into the stands and beat up a fan: "He said later he wasn't really mad at the fan, but wanted to get arrested so he could take his hangover out of the hot sun."

That 1930 season was not an aberration. It was the fourth year in five that Wilson had led the league in home runs, and he'd driven in 159 runs the year before. He had hit at least .313 every year since joining the Cubs. In '30, in addition to setting the home run and RBI records,

CUBS CAREER	
Games:	850
Runs:	652
Hits:	1,017
Home runs:	190
Runs batted in:	768
Batting average:	.322
Stolen bases:	34

Wilson became the first—and still only—National Leaguer with 50 home runs and 200 hits in the same season. He became the first 20th-century Cub to smash three home runs in one game (July 26, 1930), and to hit for the cycle (June 23, 1930).

With input from Joe McCarthy, who was about to be named Cubs manager, the Chicago club drafted Wilson from Toledo in October 1925. McCarthy got five fine years out of his 5-6 slugger despite Wilson's rambunctious behavior.

When the Cubs lost the World Series in 1929 (with Wilson losing two key fly balls in the sun), then didn't win the pennant in 1930, they let McCarthy go. His successor, Rogers Hornsby, had no patience with Wilson, punishing him with benchings and insisting he take more pitches. Wilson's numbers fell shockingly in 1931. The next year, he was playing in Brooklyn, and by 1935, he was out of the majors before his 35th birthday.

● **Outfield** *1992-2004*

Sammy Sosa

He's the only man ever to break the 60-homer mark three times.

On March 30, 1992, the Cubs traded George Bell, an established slugger who'd hit 25 home runs for them the year before, to the White Sox. They got Sammy Sosa.

Who could have guessed that the 23-year-old with a .228 career average, the kid that owner George W. Bush's Texas team had shipped to the Sox after 84 at-bats, would become:

—The Cubs' first great Latin player, and one of the most popular figures in sports.

—The only man ever to break the once-sacrosanct 60-homer mark three times, a man who would hit 66 in 1998 and not even win his league's home run title.

—Part of a home run race that would send Maris-Mantle to obscurity, a joyful contest that would put his duel with Mark McGwire on the front pages and bring fans back into baseball parks after a strike that had soured so many on the game.

—The man who'd sprint past Ernie Banks' career record for homers as a Cub.

The Cubs couldn't have known. As the Sporting News reported, "The trade of Bell ... was general manager Larry Himes' first move at cutting clubhouse problems and payroll." Sosa, it said, had a strong arm.

Who could have known about the home run hop? Who could have envisioned the post-homer kisses blown via cable TV to his mother in the Dominican Republic, the heart tap, the great smile? Who could have imagined the circling pregame sprint to right field to the roars of Wrigley Field crowds?

Sammy Sosa couldn't have known. This is a man who dropped out of school to earn money for his widowed mother and six siblings. He sold oranges and shined shoes. He played only enough baseball to be spotted by a scout and signed for $3,500.

A glance through Sosa's accomplishments would include his home runs, but also his early baserunning. He became the first Cub with a 30-30 (steals and home runs) season. Then he did it again.

Of course, it's the power numbers that will land him in the Hall of Fame. He was the first National Leaguer to have six consecutive 40-homer seasons and nine straight 100-RBI years. And only Sosa, in the long history of the game, has had three three-homer games in one season.

At 2004's end, he was seventh all-time in home runs. Next on the list: He finally catches McGwire.

Also at season's end, after walking out on the team on the final day, it seemed the increasingly unhappy Sammy had worn out his welcome in Chicago. By late January of 2005, Sosa appeared on his way to Baltimore in a trade.

● **Starting pitcher** *1904-12, 1916*

Mordecai "Three Finger" Brown

T y Cobb called his curveball "the most devastating pitch I ever faced." Mordecai Brown credited it to his lack of an index finger: "It gave me a firmer grip on the ball so I could spin it over the hump. It gave me a greater dip."

He was a small child, playing on the family farm in Indiana, when his hand got caught in a feed grain-cutting machine that his older brother was operating. Doctors had to amputate his index finger below the second joint. They were able to save the injured pinky finger, but it would be unusable.

Then, with his right hand still splinted, accident-prone Mordecai fell. His middle finger was mangled.

Still, Brown became a Hall of Famer as a righthanded pitcher.

CUBS CAREER
Games: 346
Won-Lost: 188-85
Earned-run average: 1.80
Innings pitched: 2,329
Hits allowed: 1,879
Strikeouts: 1,043
Bases on balls: 445
Shutouts: 48

It was the dead ball era, to be sure. Home runs were rare and scores were low, but Brown ranked with Christy Mathewson as the leading pitcher in the pitching-strong league and the leader of the magnificent Cubs staffs that brought the team its only World Series championships.

He was born Mordecai Peter Centennial Brown, the third name a recognition of the year, 1876. History knows him as "Three Finger." To the sporting press of the time, he was "Miner" Brown; he'd worked in coal mines as a young man. His teammates called him "Brownie."

The Cubs got him from St. Louis early in his career, and two years later he started on a string of six consecutive 20-win seasons. He was astoundingly stingy with runs. In 10

years with the Cubs, he had an earned-run average of 1.80, the best in team history. Over a four-year period that included three Chicago pennants, his highest ERA was 1.47. He was the first 20th-century National Leaguer to pitch four consecutive shutouts; his total of 48 for the Cubs is the franchise record.

Brown didn't throw exceptionally fast, but he had terrific control. In 1908, he won 29 games; In $312\frac{1}{3}$ innings that year, he walked just 49 batters.

At a time when pitchers were expected to finish what they started, Brown was used often enough in relief—revisionist record-keeping credits him with 13 saves in 1911— that one newspaperman dubbed him the "Royal Rescuer." Sometimes, he entered midgame without warmups.

In 10 years with the Cubs, he had an earned-run average of 1.80, the best in team history.

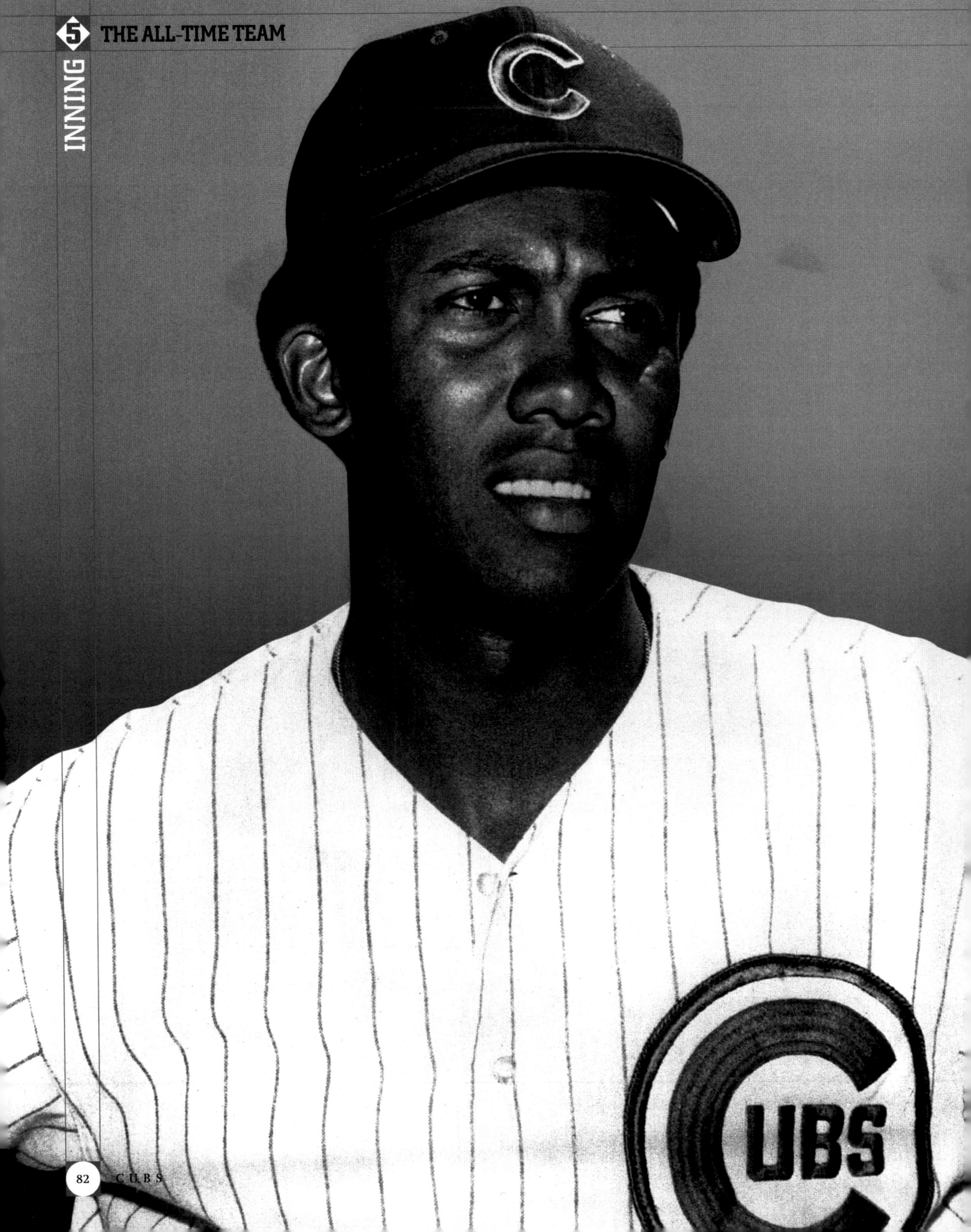
C
CUBS

● **Starting pitcher** *1966-73, 1982-83*

With Ferguson Jenkins, you knew:

—He was going to win 20 games. He did that six consecutive seasons with the Cubs, a feat that only long-ago Mordecai Brown and Clark Griffith had accomplished for the franchise.

—He was going to get the ball over the plate. He's the only major league pitcher to end his career with more than 3,000 strikeouts and fewer than 1,000 bases on balls. In 1971, he struck out 263 batters and walked just 37 (while winning 24 games).

CUBS CAREER	
Games: 401	
Won-Lost: 167-132	
Earned-run average: 3.21	
Innings pitched: 2,673⅔	
Hits allowed: 2,402	
Strikeouts: 2,038	
Bases on balls: 600	
Shutouts: 29	

—He would rack up lots of innings, and lots of strikeouts. He started 347 games for the Cubs, and struck out 2,038 for Chicago. Both are team records.

—Because he was always around the plate, and he threw lots of fastballs, he was going to give up home runs. He led the league five times while he was with the Cubs.

—The games he pitched were going to be brisk. "I used to love the afternoon games at Wrigley Field when Gibby (Bob Gibson) pitched against our Fergie Jenkins," Billy Williams said once, "because you could always plan something early for that evening. They hurried."

Jenkins was a black Canadian who didn't experience segregation until the Phillies, the team that signed him, put him at minor league teams in the South in the early '60s.

The righthander came up to the Phils as a relief pitcher, and had seen little action before the Cubs traded aging pitchers Larry Jackson and Bob Buhl for him and center fielder Adolfo Phillips. The Cubs made him a starter in 1967, and he was an instant ace. That first season in the rotation, he was 20-13. The next season, he won 20 again despite losing five 1-0 games. He won the Cy Young Award in his best year as a Cub, 1971.

"Location and changing speeds are the names of my game," he said in explaining his success. "If you can't pitch high and low, in and out in this game, you can't survive."

His string of 20-win seasons ended in 1973, and the Cubs traded him to the Rangers, thinking his arm was bad. Not quite. In his first year in Texas, he won a career-high 25 games. The Cubs eventually got Jenkins back, as a 38-year-old free agent, and he pitched his final two big-league seasons in 1982 and 1983 as a Cub.

'If you can't pitch high and low, in and out in this game, you can't survive.'

Ferguson Jenkins

Starting pitcher *1926-41; coach, 1951-53, 1960*

Charlie Root

Did he or didn't he? And does it really matter?

Charlie Root is part of one of the enduring (and perhaps endearing) legends of baseball. This much is fact: In Game 3 of the 1932 World Series, Babe Ruth of the Yankees, the most famous player in baseball, was at bat against Charlie Root of the Cubs in the fifth inning. The score was 4-4. Ruth made some sort of gesture with his hand, then hit the next pitch over the wall in deep center field.

Did Ruth point to the spot, calling his shot? The story lives on, although most of the principals have said it didn't happen that way. The consensus is that Root was a hard-throwing pitcher with a nasty disposition and that Ruth knew it, and would not have risked taunting him.

Root was prime among the scoffers. "If he had pointed to the stands," Root said later, "he'd have gone down on his fanny."

That storied moment aside, Root had much more success than failure. He was one of manager Joe McCarthy's wise acquisitions. A sidearming sinker-ball pitcher whose previous big-league experience was an unimpressive stint with the St. Louis Browns in 1923, he had, in the words of one writer, "blinding speed, and his curve cracks like amplified static on a sultry night."

Root, who posted 26 victories in 1927, wound up as the only man to win 200 games for the Cubs. Forty-two of the righthander's victories came in relief—he was 8-0 out of the bullpen in 1937.

His 3,137⅓ innings and 605 games for the Cubs are franchise records. His 16-year career in Chicago—no one has pitched nearly as long for the team—spanned four Cubs pennant winners.

Alas, Root and his team didn't do well in those four Series tries. The Cubs totaled just three wins, none of them credited to Root. In addition to the Ruth homer, Root was part of another ignominious and well-chronicled Series incident. In the seventh inning of Game 4 in 1929, he had a three-hitter and an 8-0 lead. A Cubs win would have tied the Series. But Philadelphia teed off on Root, the bullpen couldn't stop the rally, and the A's scored 10 runs and won the game. The Athletics wrapped up the title in Game 5.

Root is the only man to win 200 games for the Cubs.

● **Starting pitcher** *1913-21*

James "Hippo"
Vaughn

The best lefthanded pitcher in Cubs history.

He's best known for a couple of hours of baseball. His larger accomplishment was what he did over nine seasons: He established himself as the best lefthanded pitcher in Cubs history.

First, the game that made Hippo Vaughn famous.

It was May 2, 1917, at Weeghman Park, what's now Wrigley Field. The Cubs were playing the Cincinnati Reds, Vaughn of Chicago pitching against Fred Toney. They went nine innings with neither team scoring— or even getting a hit. The Reds, who had stacked their lineup with righthanded hitters against lefty Vaughn, had hit just one ball out of the infield, a short popup to center.

The teams went to the 10th. With one out, Cincinnati shortstop Larry Kopf grounded a ball between first and second, and the Vaughn no-hit-

ter was gone. One out later, Vaughn induced a fly ball to center fielder Cy Williams. It should have ended the inning, but Williams dropped the ball. Kopf went to third. The next batter, former Olympian Jim Thorpe, hit a dribbler down the third base line. Vaughn went for the ball, but he clearly had no shot at perhaps the world's fastest man sprinting to first base. He threw to the catcher, Art Wilson, in time to get Kopf, but Wilson missed the ball.

Toney got his no-hitter and the win. Vaughn got lasting fame along with him.

There was much more, however, to this man whose nickname derived from his big body and ungainly running form. He'd had just modest success with New York

CUBS CAREER	
Games:	305
Won-Lost:	151-104
Earned-run average:	2.33
Innings pitched:	2,216⅓
Hits allowed:	1,971
Strikeouts:	1,138
Bases on balls:	621
Shutouts:	35

and Washington in the American League and was back in the minors at Kansas City when the Cubs obtained him late in the 1913 season.

He went on to record 151 victories as a Cub, winning at least 17 seven years in a row, winning 20 five times. On the all-time franchise list, he is second in shutouts with 35. In 1918, he led the league in victories, shutouts, innings, strikeouts and ERA, winning 22 games in a season shortened because of World War I (the Cubs played just 129 games).

In the '18 World Series against the Red Sox, he pitched three marvelous games, giving up a total of three runs. He lost two of those starts. The winner in the first game was another pretty good lefthander, name of Babe Ruth.

● **Starting pitcher** *1905-13*

Ed Reulbach

ere's a feat that has never been duplicated, and certainly won't be in the era of five-man starting rotations:

In 1908, in the last days of a heated pennant race that the Cubs ultimately would win, righthander Ed Reulbach started, finished and won both games of a doubleheader against Brooklyn—and didn't allow a run. Notching two complete-games victories in one day has been achieved more than 50 times by major league pitchers—all before 1927—but no one but Big Ed tossed two shutouts.

Those were among four consecutive shutouts he threw that September, leading the Cubs into a World Series that turned out to be the last one they've won.

Pitching 18 innings in one day wasn't unprecedented for this big man of remarkable endurance. In 1905, he'd gone that long against the Cardinals in a complete-game 2-1 victory. Two months later, he defeated the Phillies by the same score—in 20 innings.

Reulbach was a man of unusual background, especially for his time. He'd studied engineering at Notre Dame and medicine at the University of Vermont, playing college ball under his own name and in the minor leagues under aliases. By the time the Cubs had tracked him down under his various names and signed him, he was already seasoned, and it showed—he won 18 games in his rookie year, 1905. The next season, he began a remarkable string. He led the league in winning percentage from 1906 through 1908, winning 60 and losing just 15 for those pennant-winning teams. In 1909, he had a 14-game winning streak.

The 1906 Cubs were one of just eight teams in history with four pitchers who won 15 games and had winning percentages of .667 or

> ## His best World Series game was his first, a one-hitter against the White Sox in 1906.

CUBS CAREER

Games: 280
Won-Lost: 136-64
Earned-run average: 2.24
Innings pitched: 1,865
Hits allowed: 1,459
Strikeouts: 799
Bases on balls: 650
Shutouts: 31

better—two victories for every loss. Reulbach led the way with a winning percentage of .826 (19-4 record).

His best World Series game was his first, a one-hitter against the White Sox in 1906. The next year, he beat the Tigers with a six-hitter, holding the great Ty Cobb to one single.

He had arm trouble in 1913, a year Cubs management was in turmoil and the championship team of the century's first decade was being dismantled. Chicago traded him to Brooklyn. He bounced around, joined former teammates in the soon-to-dissolve Federal League, and finally quit in 1917 after winding up at Providence of the International League.

Reulbach died on July 17, 1961—the same day as his World Series opponent of 1907 and '08, Ty Cobb.

INNING 5

Closer *1976-80*

Bruce Sutter

CUBS CAREER
Games: 300
Won-Lost: 32-30
Earned-run average: 2.40
Innings pitched: 492
Hits allowed: 371
Strikeouts: 494
Bases on balls: 149
Saves: 133

Lee Smith had more years in Chicago, and more saves. But Bruce Sutter got his 133 Cubs saves before every team had a warm-up-the-bus closer. And while he didn't exactly invent the split-finger pitch, no one has ever used it more effectively.

"Playing behind him in my first two years with the Cubs," Bill Buckner recalled several years later, "he was the biggest mismatch I have ever seen. He made good hitters miss by two feet."

Sutter didn't start out with a big reputation. The Cubs signed him out of semipro ball for $500 and sent him to the low minors, where he soon hurt his elbow. Reluctant to throw a curve or slider, which put strain on the arm, he went to Fred Martin, who'd had a short major league pitching career but was the Cubs' roving pitching coach. Martin showed him the split-finger pitch, which for those who could master it dropped sharply at the plate. It was held like the off-speed forkball thrown

by earlier late-inning specialists Lindy McDaniel and Roy Face, but thrown hard. It worked for Sutter.

"The split-finger did everything for my career," Sutter said years later. "If it wasn't for that pitch, I'd be back in Pennsylvania working in a printer's shop."

After a respectable first year in Chicago, he was spectacular in 1977. Due largely to his heroics, the Cubs were 25 games over .500 in

late June and comfortably in first place—this from a team that had been 12 under the previous year. But then Sutter went on the disabled list in early August with a knot under his right shoulder blade. The Cubs collapsed and finished fourth. Sutter's earned-run average that year was a scandalous 1.35.

Compared to the numbers that closers began to rack up in the next two decades, Sutter's saves

totals with the Cubs aren't impressive. He averaged 31 a year in his four strong seasons in Chicago. But the league leaders for those years averaged just 34. The reason: Closers in that era did more than enter for just one inning with their team ahead, as they do today. In his breakout '77 season, Sutter pitched 107 innings in 62 games.

In his five seasons as a Cub, Sutter appeared in four All-Star

'He made good hitters miss by two feet.'

Games. He averaged more than a strikeout an inning for Chicago, gave up fewer than seven hits per nine innings. He led the league in saves in 1979, took the Cubs to arbitration over his salary and won a then-stunning $700,000. He was the N.L. leader again in 1980, but the Wrigley ownership, cutting payroll in its final years, traded him to St. Louis. There, he would lead the league in saves three more times.

● **Pitcher** *1918-26*

Grover
Alexander

If you count the best pitchers of all time on your fingers, you count Grover Cleveland Alexander. There is no telling how good he could have been had he not been troubled, alcoholic and epileptic.

Baseball historian Donald Honig wrote: "He had become a multiple legend: Alexander the pitcher and Alexander the drinker. The Cubs, chronically in the second division, left him alone, even when occasionally he walked into the clubhouse listing a bit. But whatever his condition, when he went to the mound it was like Rembrandt to an easel." In his autobiography, Rogers Hornsby, who managed Alexander for half a season in St. Louis, insisted: "I'd rather have him pitch a crucial game for me drunk than anyone I've ever known sober. He was that good."

Alexander's first and best years were with the Phillies. He won 30 or more games three times, and his earned-run average those years went no higher than 1.86. But the Phils made him available, at age 31, because he was about to be drafted to serve in World War I.

Indeed, he was, and he came

CUBS CAREER	
Games:	242
Won-Lost:	128-83
Earned-run average:	2.84
Innings pitched:	1,884⅓
Hits allowed:	1,919
Strikeouts:	614
Bases on balls:	268
Shutouts:	24

'I'd rather have him pitch a crucial game for me drunk than anyone I've ever known sober. He was that good.'

back a changed man after seeing heavy fighting with the American Expeditionary Force in France. It's unclear how much of a problem his drinking and his seizures were before the war, but they clearly affected him on his return.

Still, he gave the Cubs 128 wins, and he was in a Chicago uniform for the landmark 300th victory of his career. He succeeded in part because of remarkable command of his pitches. He won 27 games for the Cubs in 1920, and three years later, when he was a 22-game winner, he walked just 30 batters in 305 innings.

"Pete" Alexander's control of his own life, however, didn't match that on the mound. In 1926, he didn't get along with new manager Joe McCarthy (he said he wasn't "taking orders from a bush-league manager"). The Cubs first suspended him, then released him on waivers to the Cardinals, setting up his most famous moment. At age 39, he won two games in the World Series against the Yankees, then, in relief in Game 7, struck out Tony Lazzeri with the bases loaded in the seventh inning and went on to save the game.

With his characteristic smooth delivery, he pitched until he was 43. His 373 total wins tie him with Christy Mathewson for third all-time, behind only Cy Young and Walter Johnson.

Eight years after his retirement, he was elected to the Hall of Fame, the first former Cub so honored.

In 1952, two years after Alexander's death, Ronald Reagan portrayed him in the movie *The Winning Team*.

Pitcher *1939-47*

Claude
Passeau

D on Larsen's perfect game in 1956 will stand as the best-ever World Series pitching performance until someone throws another. There have been four one-hitters— the first by the Cubs' Ed Reulbach and the second by Claude William Passeau, also of the Cubs.

On October 5, 1945, in Game 3 against Detroit, Passeau gave up a clean single to Rudy York in the second inning—and allowed no other hits, facing just 28 batters in a 3-0 victory. The Tigers' only other runner, who reached on a walk in the sixth, was eliminated by a double play.

Back at Wrigley Field for Game 6,

As a Cub, he won 124 games with an earned-run average of less than three.

Passeau was on his way to a similar performance. He'd given up just two hits, one a scratch single, when a line drive in the sixth inning tore off a fingernail on his right hand. He couldn't pitch through that. The Cubs won the game, but wore out their pitching staff, and lost decisive Game 7. It was the seventh straight World Series the Cubs had lost.

Passeau's performance in the Series was not a surprise. He'd won 17 games in '45, his seventh consecutive effective season since the Cubs got him from the Phillies. Playing for dreadful teams in Philadelphia, he'd had losing records, but as a Cubs pitcher he won 124 games with an earned-run average of less than three.

A solidly built man who stood 6-3, he had a mean slider and a mound demeanor to match. Once, in a fracas with the Dodgers, he ripped Brooklyn manager Leo Durocher's shirt. He was known to throw inside at batters with any provocation. He was a slow worker on the mound, forever fidgeting with his uniform.

Passeau grew up in rural Mississippi and went to college there, playing semipro ball under assumed names much of the time. After he became a professional, the righthander kicked around the minor league systems of several organizations before Pittsburgh brought him to the majors.

As a Cub, he pitched in three All-Star Games. The first time, he was the victim of one of the most celebrated blows in All-Star history, Ted Williams' three-run homer that won the 1941 game with two out in the bottom of the ninth. That was in Briggs Stadium in Detroit, where Claude Passeau would pitch his World Series gem four seasons later.

CUBS CAREER
Games: 292
Won-Lost: 124-94
Earned-run average: 2.96
Innings pitched: 1,914⅔
Hits allowed: 1,919
Strikeouts: 754
Bases on balls: 474
Shutouts: 23

● **Pitcher** *1986-92, 2004-present*

Greg Maddux

Maddux shows there's more to pitching than speed.

CUBS CAREER
Games: 245
Won-Lost: 111-86
Earned-run average: 3.43
Innings pitched: 1,654⅔
Hits allowed: 1,570
Strikeouts: 1,088
Bases on balls: 488
Shutouts: 14

It's not that the Cubs didn't know he was good. After the 1992 season, Greg Maddux had been their leading winner for five consecutive years and was the reigning Cy Young Award winner. But on a cold day in the winter of his free agency, the Cubs let him get away. The only issue was money.

Before Maddux came home in 2004 and got career victory No. 300 in a Cubs uniform, he had won 194 games as an Atlanta Brave. In his first year back, Maddux, at 38, won 16 games—tied for high on a club with four hard-throwing, big-reputation young starters. His 111 victories as a Cub through 2004 were the 16th highest in club history—even without those 11 center-cut years spent in Atlanta.

Just the 22nd pitcher in major league history to hit the 300 milestone, Maddux finished 2004 with 305 wins.

Even more remarkable: The '04 season was the record 17th in a row he'd won at least 15 games. Only Ty Cobb's 23 consecutive .300-hitting years (50 or more games) compares favorably as a combination of effectiveness and durability.

The secret is not a large and powerful physique. His 6-foot frame makes him small by

modern pitcher standards. But: "He's an athlete," Cubs manager Dusty Baker says. "He can run, he can field his position (he has 13 Gold Gloves), he can hit and he can pitch."

Maddux shows there's more to pitching than speed. Former Cubs pitcher-turned-writer Jim Brosnan once said, "I've never seen him throw a ball straight."

From Maddux himself: "I could probably throw harder if I wanted, but why? When they're in a jam, a lot of pitchers try to throw harder. Me, I try to locate better."

Oddly, this future Hall of Famer won 20 games only twice in his first 19 years—his last season before leaving the Cubs and his first with the Braves. He could have had 20 in 1989 (after clinching the East Division title for the Cubs with No. 19), but manager Don Zimmer chose to save Maddux for the playoffs. Alas, the Giants knocked him around and the Cubs didn't make the World Series.

At a Wrigley Field ceremony honoring Maddux for his 300 victories, Cubs general manager Jim Hendry said, "All 300 ... should have been with the Cubs."

Right.

● **Backup closer**
1980-87

Lee Smith

Smith gave the Cubs five consecutive seasons of 29 or more saves,

outfielder George Hendrick) and wasn't averse to sending the other team a message with a close pitch.

He gave the Cubs five consecutive seasons of 29 or more saves, trudging in from the bullpen 60-plus times each year. His best Chicago season was 1983, when he had a league-leading 29 saves and a 1.65 earned-run average despite being charged with 10 losses. His worst moment came the next year, in Game 4 of the N.L. Championship Series, when San Diego's Steve Garvey victimized him with a ninth-inning, game-winning home run.

All told, by the winter of 1987 Lee Smith had set still-extant Cubs records for relief appearances (452) and saves (180). And then they traded him to the Red Sox.

It was new general manager Jim Frey's first deal in a succession of bad ones. Red Sox fans who heard about the trade on the radio called Boston newspapers and Fenway Park to see if the news was a hoax. "Heist," the papers called the deal. The Cubs got pitchers Calvin Schiraldi and Al Nipper. Those two stayed in Cubs uniforms long enough to win 14 games between them, lose 23, and be shipped out of town.

There were whispers that Smith had lost the steam on his fastball, that he had back problems, knee problems, attitude problems. No problem. He gave the Red Sox and several other teams in both leagues eight more years of world-class relief pitching.

The Cubs, at least, developed one of the best relief pitchers of all time, the man with more career saves than anyone. They'd convinced him, in his minor league days, to convert from the starting role he wanted, and forced him to learn his craft in a hitters' park.

Dusty Baker would one day wish he had someone like Lee Smith to call on late in the game for the Cubs. But this dry understatement about Smith came when both were still playing:

"I don't run from anybody," Baker said, "but the general opinion around the National League is that you're in no real hurry to get to him."

Smith was a product of the Cubs' farm system who became a key member of the bullpen at age 23. Soon, he was the best closer in the league, a hulking presence, 6-6 and close to 250 pounds. He threw extremely hard ("They should make Lee Smith pitch from second base," said Cardinals

trudging in from the bullpen 60-plus times each year.

Catcher *1966-73, 1976-77*

Randy Hundley

"The first and original," say the ads for Randy Hundley's Fantasy Baseball Camp. Hundley always was ahead of his time.

They called him "The Rebel" because of his Virginia accent, but Randy Hundley was different in more significant ways.

After discovering that foul tips could break his fingers, he adopted a revolu-

tionary style of catching, one-handed with his right hand behind his back. And he invented a glove to make it work.

Pre-Hundley, a catcher's mitt resembled a stiff pillow with a depression in the middle. His glove was split and flexible, like a first baseman's.

It was effective. Hundley became the Cubs' best catcher since Gabby Hartnett, succeeding 47 others in 26 years—end-of-career types like Jim Hegan, flashes in the pan like Harry Chiti, characters like Joe Garagiola, memorable names like Facundo Barragan and Merritt Ranew. Once he came to the Cubs (from the Giants organization, with Bill Hands), Hundley immediately became a fixture—to a fault.

He caught 160 games one year, 149 or more four years in a row. He became the first player in history to

Once he came to the Cubs, Hundley immediately became a fixture—to a fault.

catch 150 or more games three consecutive years. Those who criticized manager Leo Durocher for overworking his regulars in 1969 pointed to Hundley as Exhibit No. 1. Among several teammates, his batting average for the key stretch in September was below .200.

Hundley in his prime was no pushover with the bat, but his most valuable assets were his defense and handling of pitchers. "Having

Hundley catch for you," Ferguson Jenkins once said, "was like sitting down to a steak dinner with a steak knife. Without Hundley, all you had was a fork."

He had a strong, accurate arm, and in his second year in Chicago, 1967, he set a major league record by committing only four errors. He won a Gold Glove Award. (Then Johnny Bench came along, and that was that for the Gold Glove.)

Hundley had a hot temper; when he got upset with his pitchers, he'd fire the ball back at them hard enough to knock them off the mound. But he never said anything stronger than "dadgumit" to anyone.

Hundley hurt his left knee in the spring of 1970, and played in only 82 games over two seasons. His hitting fell off badly in 1972 and '73, and the Cubs traded him to Minnesota. A comeback with the Cubs at the end of his career was unsuccessful, but as his spring-in-Arizona campers know, he has stayed around baseball, his old teammates and the Cubs.

● **First base**
1988-2000

Mark Grace

Cubs history shows inexplicable patterns. Third base was a problem for years. Lefthanded starting pitching has been a problem for always.

But name a half-dozen players, and you've named the men who have held down first base for some 60 percent of Cubs history.

Cap Anson of the 19th century was followed by Frank Chance of the early 20th. Charlie Grimm kept the spot until Phil Cavarretta came along. Ernie Banks was a fixture after he moved from shortstop. And then, for 13 years, came Mark Grace, a fine hitter, a smooth fielder, a man known for his good humor and his consistency.

The days of Grace were models of consistency. He was never a batting champion, but could be counted on to hit .300-plus. In an era of free swingers, he seldom struck out. With the glove? Keith Hernandez, his predecessor as the best in the league at the position, said this about Grace in a 1995 magazine article:

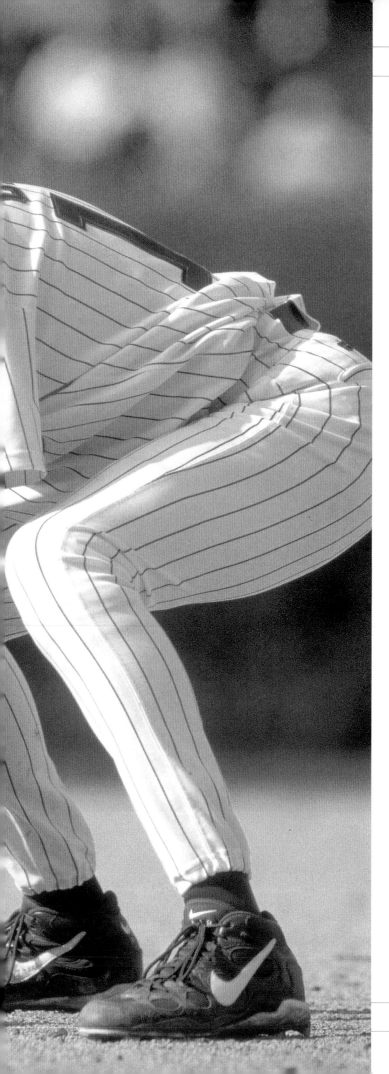

"He doesn't do anything fancy, but any ball he gets to, he handles flawlessly." Four Gold Gloves would prove that.

Grace wasn't a threat to lead the league in homers (17 was his high mark), but he was a threat nonetheless. In Sammy Sosa's 66-home run season of 1998, Sosa hit 20 in June. With Grace batting behind him most of the time, Sosa wasn't intentionally walked a single time that month.

Consistency did not mark Grace's early life. His father's railroad job moved the family frequently in his growing-up years. He was just a 24th-round draft pick by the Cubs. Three years later, though, he was in the majors, and Chicago became the first longtime home of his life. His 1988 teammates all were long gone when Grace played his last game for the Cubs. He wound up with a .308 career batting average as a Cub and is among the team's all-time top 10 in most offensive categories. Only Anson hit more doubles in a Chicago uniform.

Like Banks, Grace had a long and distinguished career in Chicago without getting to a World Series, though he was phenomenal in the Cubs' 1989 NLCS loss to the Giants, hitting .647. Unlike Banks, he got his chance. When the Cubs let him go after the 2000 season, he caught on with Arizona, and helped the Diamondbacks to a World Series title his first year there.

CUBS CAREER

Games:	1,910
Runs:	1,057
Hits:	2,201
Home runs:	148
Runs batted in:	1,004
Batting average:	.308
Stolen bases:	67

The days of Grace were models of consistency.

● **Middle infield** *1902-13; manager, 1913 and 1921*

Johnny Evers

CUBS CAREER
Games: 1,408
Runs: 742
Hits: 1,339
Home runs: 9
Runs batted in: 448
Batting average: .276
Stolen bases: 291

These are the saddest of possible words: "Tinker to Evers to Chance."

The record shows that Johnny Evers was the double-play middleman between Joe Tinker and Frank Chance for the first time on September 14, 1902. It was several years later that a New York newspa-

'Johnny Evers was a maniac on the field. You hear a lot about Cobb being like that, but Evers was even worse.'

per columnist and Giants fan, Franklin P. Adams, wrote the verse that would make the combination more famous than the individuals.

By today's reckoning, the three players didn't turn many double plays, but seemed to make them in clutch situations against their chief rivals, the Giants.

Evers was a converted shortstop

and an unlikely looking ballplayer. As a major leaguer, he weighed 125 pounds—not counting the chip on his shoulder. By all accounts, Evers was mouthy and tough, on opponents and even his teammates. Contemporary Bill Wambsganss said many years later, "Johnny Evers ... was a maniac on the field. You hear a lot about Cobb being like that, but Evers was even worse." Evers and double-play partner Tinker came to blows one day and didn't speak to each other for years, except when necessary on the field.

Still, they worked together well. They're credited with being pioneers at switching who would cover second on a steal attempt, and at decoying runners.

Offensively, Evers was a singles hitter whose main weapons were

his speedy legs.

After eight strong years with the Cubs, multiple disasters hit Evers in 1910. The automobile he was driving crashed, killing a friend of his. Evers broke his leg sliding, knocking him out of that year's World Series. At the same time, he was suffering big financial losses, and wound up suffering a nervous breakdown that cost him most of the 1911 season.

Evers became playing manager of the Cubs in 1913 after headstrong owner Charles Murphy fired Frank Chance. He finished third, with his fiery personality getting him in trouble with his players and with umpires; he was constantly being thrown out of games. Murphy canned Evers, too, and "the Crab" went on to spark the 1914 "Miracle Braves" to the pennant and World Series championship, leading the league's second basemen in fielding percentage.

Stan Hack

One of the many "if only" moments in the Cubs' post-season history:

The Cubs needed to win Game 6 of the 1935 World Series to force a decisive seventh game. With the score tied in Detroit in the ninth inning, Stan Hack led off with a triple. He stayed there through one batter, then two, then three, including pitcher Larry French. The Cubs lost the game and the Series.

The story goes that years later, visiting the ballpark in Detroit, Hack went out to third base "to see if I'm still there."

Stan Hack always could hit in the World Series, and had plenty of chances to prove it. He was in four, the only player to span the 1932, '35, '38 and '45 pennant winners.

He was a constant for 16 seasons with the Cubs, the only team he ever played for in the majors after just one year in the minors. He was their solid-fielding third baseman, their basestealing threat, their smiling, good-natured presence.

He also was an amazingly consistent lefthanded hitter who became the Cubs' leadoff man. He never hit

Hack was the only player to span the 1932, '35, '38 and '45 pennant winners.

less than .282 as an everyday player. His best average, .323, was in 1945. He never hit 10 home runs in a year, but scored more than 100 runs seven times. Twice, he led the league in stolen bases. And he batted .400 in four All-Star Games.

He ran up a .348 batting average through those four World Series losses—47 points above his lifetime average. He still holds the team record for most walks in a career, is second to Cap Anson in singles and is among the top 10 in many other categories. He played more games at third base as a Cub than anyone except Ron Santo.

Easygoing "Smilin' Stan" never was a source of controversy in his playing days, but was thrust into one when owner Phil Wrigley fired Phil Cavarretta in spring training of

1954 and made Hack manager. Succeeding his old pal and teammate, Hack did no better. Pitcher Johnny Klippstein once described him as "too nice to be a manager." His teams finished seventh, sixth and eighth, and Wrigley dumped him and general manager Wid Matthews.

It's unclear why Hack isn't in the Hall of Fame, or ever even came close, while George Kell, a talented third baseman with similar consistency and longevity, is in the Hall. Hack's accomplishments were as good or better than Kell's in most respects.

CUBS CAREER	
Games:	1,938
Runs:	1,239
Hits:	2,193
Home runs:	57
Runs batted in:	642
Batting average:	.301
Stolen bases:	165

● **Outfield** *1949-55*

Big ol' No. 9 is remembered as the best and most popular player on some bad Cubs teams, but that doesn't do him justice. He was a prodigious slugger whose numbers could—should—have been much better.

Sauer hit more home runs per at-bat in a Cubs uniform than Hack Wilson, more than Ernie Banks, more than anyone (minimum 1,500 at-bats) until Sammy Sosa. Unfortunately, he didn't start his Chicago slugging until he was 32. He wound up with more home runs after that age than long-career, long-ball hitters Banks and Frank Robinson (and the same total as Reggie Jackson).

What happened? Sauer originally was in the Yankees organization, signed by the same scout who discovered Lou Gehrig, Whitey Ford and other stars-to-be. He lost nearly two seasons to World War II, got buried in the minors, and had only a handful of major league games before 1948, when he set a Cincinnati franchise record with 35

Hank Sauer

home runs. In 1949, after a slow start, he came to the Cubs with fellow outfielder—and roommate—Frankie Baumholtz. Reds general manager Warren Giles said later that trade was his biggest mistake.

After hitting 27 homers for the Cubs in '49 (and 31 overall that year), Sauer had three straight 30-homer seasons for Chicago, fell off one year, then hit 41.

His best season was 1952, when he smashed 18 home runs in the team's first 50 games, and wound up leading the league with 37 homers and 121 runs batted in. His homer won the All-Star game that

year, and he was named the league's Most Valuable Player, even though the Cubs wound up fifth (the best finish of his Chicago years).

They called Hank Sauer "The Mayor of Wrigley Field." Fans would toss chewing tobacco to him after homers, or hang packs of it down from the bleachers on fishing lines, and he collected enough to supply the whole club. He didn't need it all; he never chewed off the field.

People joked about his lack of mobility in the field—he tore up his knee a couple of years before coming to the Cubs—but he caught about anything he could reach.

Sauer was traded before the 1956 season to the Cardinals, then finished his career with the Giants.

'The Mayor of Wrigley Field.'

CUBS CAREER
Games: 862
Runs: 498
Hits: 852
Home runs: 198
Runs batted in: 587
Batting average: .269
Stolen bases: 6

● **Outfield** *1928-35; coach, 1941-43*

In midseason 1930, a year the Cubs put together perhaps the best collection of hitters in their history, the Sporting News ran a headline above a head-and-shoulders picture of Kiki Cuyler. "CUBS' ACCELERATOR FOR PENNANT DRIVE," it said.

"Kiki this year has been leading the National League in stolen bases and in scoring runs," the article said, "and has been hitting around the .360 mark continuously, but that's nothing new for him."

It was not. Cuyler began in the majors with Pittsburgh, and was a World Series hero after his double against Walter Johnson won the seventh game for the Pirates in 1925. But in 1927, after feuding with his manager, he was benched by the Pirates, kept out of that year's Series and then traded to Chicago. He fit right into a team that fit right into an offensive era.

He joined Hack Wilson and Riggs Stephenson in an outfield that averaged a collective .340 over the next three years, in which the Cubs finished third, first and second. Cuyler led the league in stolen bases each of those years. No other

Cub has ever led in steals three times, consecutive or not. In 1930, hitting in front of Wilson and his 191 RBIs, Cuyler scored 155 runs—just one off Rogers Hornsby's club record—and drove in 134.

In contrast to his many swashbuckling teammates, Cuyler was a quiet sort who was valedictorian of his high school class, a championship dancer and a nondrinker. "Kiki" is a play on his last name, and less a mouthful than the name his grew up with in Michigan: Hazen Shirley Cuyler.

By whatever name, he was a consistent hitter and strong-armed outfielder. To this day, only six players have amassed three or more seasons with 100 runs scored, 100 runs batted in, 30 steals. Two are active: Barry Bonds and Carlos Beltran. The other three, like Cuyler, are in the Hall of Fame: Ty Cobb, George Sisler and Honus Wagner.

When Cuyler, a .321 career hitter who once had 26 triples in a season, died in 1950, Jack Doyle, a longtime scout for the Cubs, called him "a righthanded Ty Cobb"—though gentlemanly Cuyler didn't have Cobb's fierceness.

CUBS CAREER

Games: 949

Runs: 665

Hits: 1,199

Home runs: 79

Runs batted in: 602

Batting average: .325

Stolen bases: 161

No other Cub has ever led the league in steals three times, consecutive or not.

● **Pinch hitter** *1934-53; manager, 1951-53*

Phil
Cavarretta

He hit grand slams in three decades as a Cub.

He's identified with generations of Cubs—starting as a teenager playing with Charlie Root and Gabby Hartnett and winding up a manager—and teammate—of Ernie Banks. His contributions matched his longevity.

Cavarretta was a Chicago native, the son of Italian immigrants, who joined the team when he was just 18 and weighed about 150 pounds. Babe Ruth, who wound up his career with the Braves, said to him before a game in 1935: "Eighteen years old? You should be in high school!"

But he won a 1-0 game for the Cubs in 1934 with a homer in his first start and became the regular first baseman, replacing manager Charlie Grimm, on the '35 team that won the pennant. That infield was full of memorable Cubs—Stan Hack, Billy Jurges, Billy Herman, Cavarretta.

His best year was the season of the Cubs' last pennant, 1945, when he led the league with a .355 average and was named its Most Valuable Player.

Cavarretta was a fine fielder at first base, and when he wasn't starting, he was a clutch hitter off the bench (leading the league in pinch hits in '51). He wasn't a great home run producer, but he could deliver the long ball at key times. He hit grand slams in three decades as a Cub, the last as a pinch hitter off Hall-of-Famer-to-be Robin Roberts. His last Cubs home run came when manager Cavarretta sent up pinch hitter Cavarretta against Murry Dickson of the Pirates in 1952. It won the game.

Throughout his career, his teammates regarded "Philibuck"—a hot-tempered, gung-ho hustler—as a team leader, so it was not surprising that owner Phil Wrigley saw the makings of a manager in him, even before he finished playing. It was as a dugout leader who still was on the field that he had the center field bleachers closed at Wrigley Field to provide a better backdrop for hitters.

The circumstances of his departure are still cited as an object lesson in the dangers of being too honest. In March 1954, he told Wrigley that the Cubs needed better players or they'd be a losing team. Wrigley interpreted that as defeatism, and Phil Cavarretta became the first manager ever fired in spring training.

Stan Hack took over. Sure enough, the Cubs had a losing team, finishing seventh in an eight-team league.

CUBS CAREER	
Games:	1,953
Runs:	968
Hits:	1,927
Home runs:	92
Runs batted in:	896
Batting average:	.292
Stolen bases:	61

INNING 6 The

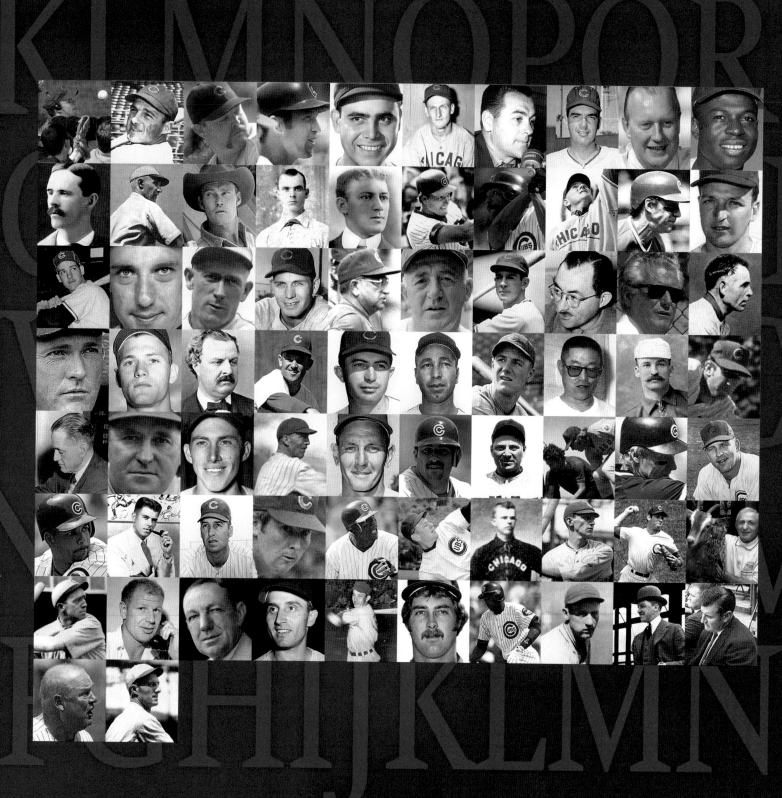

Cubs, A to Z

Alou, Moises *(2002-04)*

Signed as a free agent in December 2001 to take some of the offensive burden off Sammy Sosa, Moises Alou was a disappointment in an injury-tainted 2002 season, more of what the Cubs expected in 2003 and more than anyone had a right to expect in 2004 when, at age 38, he contributed 39 home runs and 106 runs batted in. Even if the glowering, clutch-hitting Alou had not stared down Father Time in '04, he forever is assured a spot in Cubs lore. Something about a postseason incident in '03 that reportedly made some of the papers.

Altman, George

(1959-62, 1965-67)

He had three pro baseball careers. Like Ernie Banks, outfielder George Altman began playing for pay with the Kansas City Monarchs of the Negro leagues. He made the majors at a time when black players were still a distinct minority, and he wound up as one of the first successful American players in Japan. A streaky hitter, he batted .303 and .318 for bad Cubs teams in 1961-62. Altman had a two-homer game against Sandy Koufax in '61. After his baseball career, he dealt in commodities on the Chicago Board of Trade.

Baker, Dusty

(manager, 2003-present)

Fresh from taking the Giants to the 2002 World Series, he signed on to manage a Cubs team that had finished 67-95 in '02. Vowing to do away with the team's image as "lovable losers," Dusty Baker succeeded on two fronts—he made the Cubs aggressive and edgy, not cute and cuddly, and winners, not also-rans. The 88-74 team won the 2003 N.L. Central title and came within five outs of reaching the World Series. In 2004, a year of great expectations that went unrealized, he nonetheless managed the club to a second consecutive winning season (stratosphere to which the Cubs had not soared since 1971-72).

Baker, Gene

(1953-57)

He was the first black player signed by the Cubs, in 1950, but Gene Baker languished nearly four seasons as shortstop for the team's Los Angeles farm club. He and Ernie Banks joined the Cubs on the same day in September 1953,

Baker switching to second base to accommodate Banks. Baker, the better known of the two prospects. made his big-league debut three days later than Banks. They started alongside each other for the first time on September 22 of '53 and were second-short partners until Baker was traded to Pittsburgh in '57. Baker hit .266 with fair power for the Cubs.

Barnes, Ross

(1876-77)

Second baseman Ross Barnes hit the first home run in major league history —and wound up with a career total of two. He was the Cubs' first batting champion, at .404, in the National League's first year, 1876. Under today's rules, that average translates to .429; that season, a walk was scored as a hitless at-bat. Then again, that year a ball that hit fair between home and the corner bases and then rolled foul was a fair ball—and those hits were Barnes' specialty. When the rule changed in 1877, he batted .272.

Bartman, Steve

(2003)

The Cubs lead the 2003 NLCS, three games to two, and are ahead, 3-0, in Game 6, with one out in the Florida eighth, a runner on second. Luis Castillo hits Mark Prior's full-count pitch toward the stands along the left field line at Wrigley Field. Moises Alou leaps, reaches into the crowd ... and finds the ball deflected by a fan. The Cubs collapse, lose the game, lose the next game, lose their chance to reach the World Series. Cubs loyalist Steve Bartman, 26, who interfered, is pelted with beer and jeers and receives death threats. He is forced into hiding.

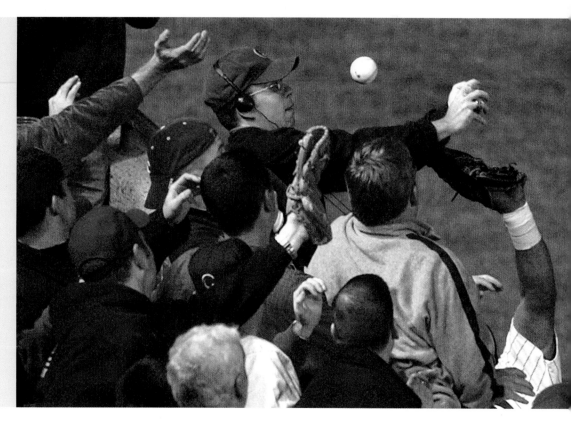

Baumholtz, Frankie

(1949, 1951-55)

An excellent athlete who also played pro basketball, Frankie Baumholtz was a fine gap hitter who challenged Stan Musial for the 1952 N.L. batting title but wound up second at .325. In a season-finale gimmick, Musial pitched to one hitter, Baumholtz, who reached on an error after turning around and batting righthanded. Baumholtz hit .306 the next year. In his last season with the Cubs, 1955, he led the league in pinch hitting (.405). Baumholtz, acquired from Cincinnati in a 1949 trade that also netted Hank Sauer, lost four prime years because of Navy duty in World War II.

Beck, Rod *(1998-99)*

One of the franchise's most important signees of the free-agent era, "The Shooter" came to Chicago in 1998 with 199 career saves for San Francisco, more than anyone ever amassed for the Cubs. Hair flowing out of his cap and mustache framing his chin, Rod Beck piled up 51 more saves that season, typically in heart-stopping, five-up-and-three-down fashion. In his 81st and final appearance, he finished the Cubs' wild-card playoff win over the Giants by getting Joe Carter to pop up in Carter's last major league at-bat.

Beckert, Glenn *(1965-73)*

He'll always be linked with Don Kessinger, his double-play partner all nine years he played second base for the Cubs. Players called Glenn Beckert "Stonefingers" because he didn't have the "soft" hands the game prizes, but he won a Gold Glove and was a four-time All-Star Game participant. After young second base star Ken Hubbs died in an airplane crash in 1964, the Cubs converted Beckert, a minor league shortstop. His best year was 1971, when he hit .342. Difficult to strike out, he fanned only 20 times in 643 at-bats in 1968.

Bithorn, Hi *(1942-43, 1946)*

The name Hiram Bithorn reappeared on mainland sports pages for the first time in more than half a century in 2003 when the Expos started playing some home games in Puerto Rico. The field they used was Hiram Bithorn Stadium, named for the first Puerto Rican to play in the majors. Bithorn won 18 games for the Cubs in 1943, with seven shutouts, but faded fast. He was killed by a police officer in Mexico in 1952 at age 35. Bithorn once threw at provocative Leo Durocher—Durocher was sitting in the Dodgers' dugout at the time.

Borowy, Hank *(1945-48)*

It's still unclear why in late July of 1945 the Yankees let go of the best pitcher in the wartime American League, but the Cubs didn't look a workhorse in the mouth. Hank Borowy, 10-5 for the Yankees in '45 before being sold to the Cubs, won 11 times in two months (with an ERA of 2.13) for his new team and the Cubs won their last pennant of the 20th century. In the '45 World Series against Detroit, he pitched a six-hit shutout in Game 1 and went 2-2 overall.

Boudreau, Lou

(1958-59 and 1961-87, broadcaster;
1960, manager)

In 1942, he'd become a big-league manager (Cleveland) at age 24; in 1960, he managed his 16th and last season in the majors, starting the year as the Cubs' radio analyst and then replacing Charlie Grimm as field boss 17 games into the season. After the Cubs finished seventh, Lou Boudreau went back to the booth, but there was no new manager—owner Phil Wrigley initiated the "College of Coaches." Called the "Good Kid," Boudreau led the Indians to their last World Series title as a player-manager in 1948.

Brewer, Jim *(1960-63)*

Lefthander Jim Brewer's Cubs career is remembered for one hit he allowed: Billy Martin broke his jaw in a fight. Brewer and the Cubs sued Martin (with the Reds at the time) for more than a million dollars. Martin cracked: "How do they want the money, cash or check?" Another line making the rounds: "And they said Martin couldn't hit lefties." Brewer eventually got a small fraction of the sum—and three operations—and later became a successful reliever for the Dodgers. He pitched 17 seasons in the majors.

Brickhouse, Jack

(1941-45 and 1947-81, broadcaster)

"Back she goes ... Way back ... Back ... Back ... Hey, Hey!" That was Hall of Fame broadcaster Jack Brickhouse's home run call, in black and white and color, for Andy Pafko, Hank Sauer, Ernie Banks, Ron Santo. It was evidence, in the words of this unpretentious, chubby-faced announcer from Peoria, that "Nothing beats fun at the old ballpark." Brickhouse wasn't the first voice on a Cubs telecast (that was Whispering Joe Wilson), but he took over when WGN began doing the games and never moved. For many years, he did both Cubs and White Sox home games.

Brock, Lou *(1961-64)* and Broglio, Ernie

(1964-66)

The names are forever paired in Cubs lore, the principals in the worst trade in Cubs history. Lou Brock was a speedy, athletic Cubs outfielder with abundant promise and a .251 batting average two months into the 1964 season; Ernie Broglio was a big righthanded pitcher who'd won 18 games for the Cardinals in 1963. The two switched teams June 15 in a six-player deal, and Brock went on to lead the Cardinals to the 1964 World Series title, break Ty Cobb's career stolen base record and land in the Hall of Fame. Broglio went on to win seven games as a Cub, lose 19, and retire with elbow problems.

Brosnan, Jim *(1954, 1956-58)*

"The Professor" did not have a memorable pitching career, but he threw the game some curves as the pioneering "tell all" baseball author. Jim Brosnan's The Long Season and Pennant Race were precursors to Jim Bouton's Ball Four, frank and frequently R-rated contrasts to traditional sugary, ghost-written baseball autobiographies. Brosnan's diary-form books frequently were scornful of other players, managers and front-office people—by name.

Brown, Brant

(1996-98, 2000)

It is a recurring theme in club history: important game, batter hits a fly ball, Cubs outfielder misses it. Brant Brown's gaffe came in Milwaukee on September 23, 1998, when the Cubs, in a hot wild-card race, were trying to protect a two-run lead in the ninth inning of a game they had led, 7-0. Rod Beck pitching, bases loaded, two out. Geoff Jenkins

hits an easy fly ball to left. Brown drops it. Three runs score, Brewers win, 8-7. The Cubs fall behind the Mets in the wild-card standings but make the postseason with a playoff victory over the Giants.

Bryant, Clay *(1935-40)*

One glorious year marked his place in Cubs history: In the pennant-winning season of 1938, he won 19 games and led the league in strikeouts (and walks). The year before, Clay Bryant was 7-0 as a reliever (9-3 overall) and won a game at Boston with a 10th-inning grand slam. A sore arm limited him to just 12 appearances over 1939 and 1940, and he was done. He stayed in baseball many more years, though, as a coach and minor league manager.

Buckner, Bill *(1977-84)*

Billy Buck came from the Dodgers off a .301 year, and he left with a .300 average for his seven-plus seasons with the Cubs. He won a batting crown in 1980. Bill Buckner had a reputation for leaving few complaints unexpressed. He and his last Cubs boss, G.M. Dallas Green, weren't mutual admirers, and Buckner was traded to Boston for Dennis Eckersley in May 1984. Buckner had a fine career but is remembered chiefly for the ground ball he didn't field for the curse-plagued Red Sox. The man who replaced him at first base for the curse-plagued Cubs: Leon Durham.

Burris, Ray

(1973-79)

He'd done little to distinguish himself in the bullpen the previous two years, but in 1975 Ray Burris was made a starter by manager Jim Marshall. He became the staff ace that season, winning 15 games. It was the first of three consecutive years of double-digit wins for Burris, who tossed four shutouts in '76.

Bush, Guy *(1923-34)*

A skinny Mississippi country boy showed up in Al Capone's town in the Roaring '20s. "I was scared," Guy Bush said. "I had heard about all the gangsters ... I had never ridden an elevator that went up and down, and I didn't know about streetcars." He did wonderfully. Bush was 152-101 as a Cub, with 34 of those victories in relief. He saved 27 games. In 1927, he pitched all 18 innings in a win at Boston. Having posted double-figure victory totals from 1926 through '32, he finally won 20 games in 1933 after fans mailed him four-leaf clovers.

Caray, Harry

(1982-97, broadcaster)

When Harry Caray sang "Take Me Out to the Ball Game" at Wrigley Field, he squinted through heavy glasses and belted out the words while sounding as if he were trying to gargle at the same time. The Cubs' television play-by-play man already was a broadcasting legend for his quarter-century announcing Cardinals games on the radio, but his act went national with the Cubs. He replaced another icon, Jack Brickhouse, a move that coincided with WGN-TV's growth to superstation status. His "Holy Cow!" expression—he invented it "so I wouldn't say something unprintable"—was famous. So was his reputation for consuming the beer he plugged.

Cardenal, Jose *(1972-77)*

He had a rep, that's for sure. He's the guy who begged off a game because, he said, his eyelid had stuck shut overnight, and missed another start because, he said, a cricket had chirped under his bed and kept him awake. The stories aside, Jose Cardenal lasted 18 years in the majors, playing for nine teams. From '72 through '76, he played beside Rick Monday in the outfield, hitting in the .290s or better each year and leading the team in stolen bases each season. He had six hits in a 14-inning game in '76.

Clarkson, John *(1884-87)*

In 1885, John Clarkson won 53 games (one of them a no-hitter), worked 623 innings and pitched 68 complete games. He won the Cubs' first game at West Side Park, also in '85, and threw a no-hitter that year as well. His workload eased, Clarkson notched 73 victories over the next two seasons. Once, he threw three shutouts in five days. He engineered a sale to Boston, his hometown, after the '87 season and enjoyed great success there, too. Among the first overhand pitchers, the Hall of Famer posted 327 major league victories.

Cey, Ron *(1983-86)*

Squatty Ron Cey didn't look, walk or run like a typical ballplayer. And critics raised eyebrows when the Cubs got "The Penguin" from the Dodgers and gave him a big contract at age 35. But Cey was a solid short-term answer to the Cubs' perennial third base problem. Even with a decade of big-league ball behind him, Cey was a key reason the '84 Cubs were so good—he led the East Division champions in homers (25) and RBIs (97).

Cole, King *(1909-12)*

Leonard "King" Cole had a spectacular start in the majors, but his success—and indeed Cole himself—would be short-lived. As a rookie in 1910, Cole had a 20-4 record and started one World Series game; in 1911, he compiled an 18-7 mark. But Cole contracted malaria, lost his effectiveness, and was traded to Pittsburgh. After pitching for the Yankees in 1914 and 1915 with so-so success, he died in the offseason of what news reports called "cancer of the lungs." He was 29 years old.

Corcoran, Larry *(1880-85)*

The star pitcher of the Chicago team that won three straight pennants as the 1880s opened was, in manager Cap Anson's words, "a very little fellow, with an unusual amount of speed, and the endurance of an Indian pony." In fact, Larry Corcoran endured as a baseball great for only five seasons before a sore arm shortened his career, and he died at 32. He won 170 games from 1880 through '84, using an underhand delivery, and he threw Chicago's first no-hitter (and then hurled two more). He also hit the team's first grand slam.

Dahlen, Bill *(1891-98)*

Bill Dahlen got hot in 1894, putting together a then-record 42-game batting streak. After 110 more years of baseball, only Joe DiMaggio, Willie Keeler and Pete Rose have exceeded that mark. Dahlen was clearly locked in—after his streak-ending game, he hit safely in the next 28 games. Manager Cap Anson called Dahlen, a shortstop, "quick as a cat." "Bad Bill" had a weakness for horse racing, and sometimes got himself thrown out of games so he could get to the track. Eventually, the umpires caught on and Dahlen couldn't be bad enough.

Connors, Chuck
(1951)

Square of jaw with eyes of steel, he carried a big stick and hit with unerring accuracy. Unfortunately, this was not in Chuck Connors' days as a Cubs first baseman; instead, it came in his TV role as Lucas McCain, the Winchester-wielding hero of *The Rifleman*. Even as a pro athlete (he played for the Boston Celtics, too), it was clear where his talent lay. One piece of evidence: He hit .239 as a Cub (in 66 games). Another: Before Brooklyn unloaded him, Branch Rickey had Connors enliven spring camp with recitations of Casey at the Bat.

Davis, Jody *(1981-88)*

The big guy from Georgia, the first stable presence behind the Wrigley plate since Randy Hundley, wound up catching more games as a Cub than anyone but Gabby Hartnett. A righthanded hitter, he walloped 17 or more homers five years in a row. He was a Gold Glove winner, a two-time All-Star Game participant and a 94-RBI contributor to the division-winning 1984 team. It wasn't Jody Davis' fault that the Cubs couldn't beat the Padres in the '84 NLCS—he hit .389 with two homers.

Dawson, Andre *(1987-92)*

A free agent after the 1986 season, longtime Expos standout Andre Dawson offered to sign a blank contract with the Cubs and let management fill in the salary. By Dawson's account, he ended up with $500,000—less than half of what he'd made the year before. "The Hawk" got a standing ovation in his first Wrigley at-bat in '87, and the cheers never stopped during a season in which Dawson (49 homers, 137 RBIs) became the first MVP from a last-place team. The right fielder had two more 100-RBI seasons for Chicago and won two of his eight Gold Gloves as a Cub. Dawson's 1988 contract, by the way, was for nearly $2 million.

Demaree, Frank
(1932-33, 1935-38)

He was a sometimes-sensational right fielder, but Frank Demaree contributed mainly with his bat. He hit .325, .350 and .324 in successive seasons. He played on all three Cubs pennant winners of the '30s, and hit two homers in the 1935 World Series. Demaree drove in 115 runs and scored 104 times in 1937. In one of their inexplicable trades, the Cubs sent Demaree, still just 28, and shortstop Billy Jurges to the Giants after the 1938 pennant year.

Dernier, Bob *(1984-87)*

Leading off for the Cubs in the first inning of the team's first postseason appearance in 39 years, Bob Dernier slashed a home run that ignited a 13-0 rout of the Padres in Game 1 of the 1984 NLCS. The Cubs were in that series in large part because of Dernier, an afterthought in the deal that brought Gary Matthews from the Phillies. The fleet center fielder could chase down long drives and was a legitimate top-of-the-order hitter. He stole 45 bases in '84, the most for a Cub since Johnny Evers in 1907, and hit .278 with 94 runs scored.

Drabowsky, Moe and Drott, Dick

(1956-60; coach, 1994)   *(1957-61)*

They were the Wood and Prior of their day, two young sensations who would lead the Cubs out of the second division. Dick Drott, with a great curveball, won 15 games in his rookie year, 1957. One of those victories came in a 15-strikeout performance against Milwaukee in which he fanned Henry Aaron three times. Drott blew out his arm, though, and won only 12 more games in the majors. Moe Drabowsky finished 13-15 in '57 and wound up 9-11 in '58. Traded away in '61, he had a 17-year career in the majors and became a valued reliever in the American League. Cubs manager Bob Scheffing said rookie Drott had "the killer instinct of a tiger and the friendliness of a lamb." Drabowsky, born in Poland, was a noted prankster. Once, while in the bullpen in Anaheim, he picked up the phone, called a number in Hong Kong and ordered a Chinese dinner. "To go," of course.

Dunston, Shawon

(1985-95, 1997)

Picked No. 1 overall in baseball's amateur draft after hitting .790 in his last year of high school ball, Shawon Dunston became a solid shortstop for the Cubs for a decade. He was a rarity at the time: a Cubs-developed position player who became a longtime regular with the club. Dunston teamed with Ryne Sandberg, and later Mark Grace, to give the Cubs years of infield quality and stability. Dunston could hit, run and field. Could he throw? Cardinals manager Whitey Herzog supplied the answer: "I know why they drafted the guy ahead of (Dwight) Gooden—he's got a better arm."

Durocher, Leo *(manager, 1966-72)*

So many stories: Getting attention as the pugnacious Gas House Gang shortstop. ... Getting more attention with his "nice guys finish last" quote. ... Cultivating the Hollywood crowd. ... Managing the 1951 "Miracle at Coogan's Bluff" Giants. ... Taking over the Cubs in '66 and saying, "This is not an eighth-place team." He's right—the club finishes 10th. ... Guiding the shoulda-been team of '69 that folded late. Did he overwork pitchers? Underuse the bench? ... Trying to dump Ernie Banks—Leo Durocher should be the No. 1 Cub. ... Feuding with writers and Jack Brickhouse. ... Ripping players in public.

Durham, Leon *(1981-88)*

It's not completely fair that Leon Durham is less than fondly remembered by Cubs fans. It wasn't his fault that the team traded the era's best relief pitcher, Bruce Sutter, to get Durham (and Ken Reitz). He does, however, bear responsibility for botching that @#$%^& ground ball: It's 1984, and the Cubs lead the Padres, 3-2, in the seventh inning of the deciding game of the NLCS. Tim Flannery grounds to first baseman Durham, who goes down on one knee to stop it. The ball somehow rolls between his legs and into right field. A run scores, with three more to follow in the inning. The Cubs do not go to the World Series.

Eckersley, Dennis
(1984-86)

Who knew where his pitching talent lay? The Chicago Tribune once said Dennis Eckersley resembled an aging hippie "who has lost his way and somehow found himself in a major league game." Still, Eckersley had been a solid starter in the American League—he won 20 games for the Red Sox in 1978—when the Cubs acquired him in late May of '84 for Bill Buckner. Eckersley won 10 games over the rest of the season, helping the Cubs to the N.L. East title. In 1987, he was traded to Oakland and converted into a closer at age 32. He excelled in his new role, amassing 390 saves as a Hall of Fame relief pitcher.

Elia, Lee
(1968; 1982-83, manager)

In April 1983, the Cubs had just lost to the Dodgers on a Lee Smith wild pitch, making their record 5-14. Fans booed. Fans spilled beer on Keith Moreland. Manager Lee Elia let his feelings be known: "Eighty-five percent of the people in this country work and the other 15 percent come out here and boo my players," he began. The rest of the speech was notable for Elia's ability to modify every noun with a particularly rude adjective. He kept his job four more months.

Ellsworth, Dick
(1958-66)

Successful lefthanded starting pitchers are to the Cubs what World Series titles are to the Cubs. Scarce. James "Hippo" Vaughn, throwing with his left arm, won 20 or more games for the Cubs five times from 1914 through 1919. No southpaw won 20 again on the North Side until Dick Ellsworth followed a 20-loss season with a superb 22-10 mark (and 2.11 ERA) in 1963. He didn't do it again, and no Cubs lefty has since. Ellsworth had three other double-digit win totals and a second 20-loss season for the Cubs, for whom he first pitched at age 18.

Elson, Bob

(1928-41, broadcaster)

In Chicago in the '30s, a quarter and an empty pack of Old Gold cigarettes would get you Bob Elson's Own Record Book, full of baseball information. "The Commander" did the first regular-season Cubs broadcasts, initiated over the protests of other National League owners. Eventually, he took his laconic style to the White Sox and, briefly, the Oakland A's. He was the first Cubs announcer named to the Hall of Fame's broadcast wing.

Elston, Don

(1953, 1957-64)

Don Elston succeeded Turk Lown as the Cubs' bullpen ace at a time when relief specialists were coming into vogue. Elston led the N.L. in games pitched in 1958 with 69 and tied teammate Bill Henry for the top spot in 1959 with 65. He fashioned a sub-3.00 ERA three times. Elston wound up with 434 relief appearances for the Cubs, second on the franchise career list behind Lee Smith's 452.

Ernaga, Frank *(1957-58)*

What a find! Outfielder Frank Ernaga became the second Cub—Paul Gillespie was the first, in 1942—to homer in his first major league at-bat. Ernaga connected against Warren Spahn, and he tripled against the future Hall of Famer his next time up. Ernaga's next three hits were a double, another homer, another triple. After eight at-bats in four games, Ernaga had five extra-base hits. Unfortunately, he could hit only lefties—and not consistently at that. Ernaga got hurt running into the Wrigley Field vines, and he wound up with just 43 career at-bats.

English, Woody *(1927-36)*

Rogers Hornsby, who had little good to say about anyone, called him "the best shortstop in the business." Elwood "Woody" English was a good player—he was named to the N.L. team for the first All-Star Game in 1933—but perhaps Hornsby was a bit too loyal to his roomie, a .286 career hitter. In 1930, though, English hit .335 and was among the elite few in baseball history with 200 hits and 100 walks in the same season. After an injury, he lost his shortstop spot to Billy Jurges, moved to third, and lost that job to Stan Hack.

Faul, Bill *(1965-66)*

He prepared for games by removing the heads of live parakeets—with his teeth. He swallowed live toads, contending they put an extra hop on his fastball. And Bill Faul hypnotized himself before pitching. Hey, it was the 1960s. Sometimes, it all worked—Faul pitched three shutouts for the Cubs in 1965. Most times, it didn't—Faul was 7-10 overall as a Cub and something less than a favorite of Leo Durocher, his manager in '66.

Flack, Max *(1916-22)*

Before there was Brant Brown, before there was Don Young, there was Max Flack, a usually reliable outfielder who dropped a third-inning fly ball in Game 6 of the 1918 World Series that allowed two Red Sox runners to score. Boston won, 2-1, clinching the Series title. There's another reason Flack is remembered: In 1922, the Cubs traded him to the Cardinals for outfielder Cliff Heathcote. The teams consummated the deal between games of a morning-afternoon Chicago-St. Louis doubleheader, and Flack and Heathcote played for their new clubs in the nightcap.

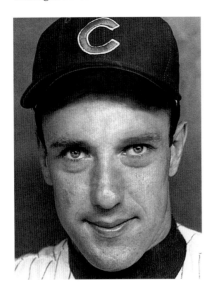

Fondy, Dee *(1951-57)*

Manager Phil Cavarretta installed Dee Fondy as the Cubs' regular first baseman, replacing ... Phil Cavarretta, who had manned the position most of the time since 1935. In 1952, his first full season in the majors, Fondy batted .300; in '53, he finished at .309 and hit 18 home runs. On April 16, 1955, he and Ernie Banks twice hit back-to-back homers in the same game. Fondy was a solid all-around player in the not-so-glorious 1950s.

Frey, Jim *(manager, 1984-86; general manager, 1987-91)*

He was the Cubs' first Manager of the Year, so named in 1984 for leading the team Dallas Green built to within eight outs of the World Series. The next year, the whole rotation went on the disabled list, and by June 1986 Green had fired his manager. After Green quit in '87, the Cubs needed a new general manager, and turned to ... Jim Frey. In that role, Frey made the especially bad decision to trade relief ace Lee Smith. Still, the Cubs won a division title (1989) on his watch as G.M.

Frisch, Frankie

(manager, 1949-51)

The Cubs finished eighth, seventh and eighth (out of eight) in Frankie Frisch's two partial seasons and one full year as Cubs manager. He got off on the wrong foot in his mouth when he declared, in 1949, "I've got one player on the team (Hank Sauer), and the rest are minor leaguers." "The Fordham Flash" hadn't inherited the '27 Yankees, but the roster did include Andy Pafko, Phil Cavarretta, Bob Rush, Dutch Leonard and Frankie Baumholtz, accomplished big-leaguers all. Bored with the second division, Frisch was known to read novels in the dugout during games.

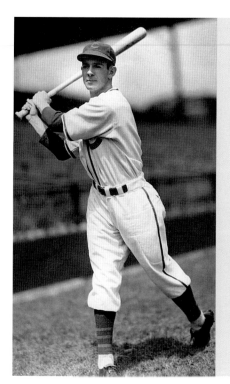

Galan, Augie

(1934-41)

A talented, though oft-injured, center fielder, Augie Galan was (a) the first major leaguer to play a 154-game schedule without grounding into a double play, (b) the first National Leaguer to hit home runs from both sides of the plate in the same game and (c) the first Cub to hit a homer in an All-Star game.

Gallagher, Jim

(1940-49, general manager)

Sportswriters can tell general managers how to run a team without being responsible for the results. Not so Jim Gallagher, a writer for the Chicago Herald-American. Owner Phil Wrigley picked him as G.M. though baseball people thought Gallagher knew no more about the game than, well, a sportswriter. The critics were right. Gallagher dealt away future Hall of Famer Billy Herman and spark-plug Eddie Stanky, among others. His most notable success

was acquiring Hank Borowy from the Yankees. Such was Gallagher's reputation that it was assumed New York's management knew something he didn't about Borowy.

Green, Dallas *(1981-87, general manager)*

Soon after the new owner of the Cubs, the Chicago Tribune Co., named Dallas Green as G.M., Green told a magazine writer: "I knew what I had here, and I didn't have crap." He remade the organization and the team. Many of the new faces came from his former team, the Phillies, which sparked some controversy. Yet ex-Phils Larry Bowa, Gary Matthews, Keith Moreland, Bob Dernier and especially Ryne Sandberg were key players in the Cubs' drive to the 1984 East Division title. The price was high to bolster the pitching staff—Green gave up Bill Buckner for Dennis Eckersley and traded Joe Carter and Mel Hall for Rick Sutcliffe—but the Cubs, 20 games under .500 in 1983, finished 31 over in '84 and just missed making the World Series.

Griffith, Clark

(1893-1900)

"The Old Fox" posted 152 victories as a Cubs pitcher, winning 20 or more games in six consecutive seasons. In 1901, he jumped to the White Sox of the newly formed American League and led the Sox to the '01 pennant in the dual role of manager/pitcher (he won 24 games). Clark Griffith played for seven big-league clubs overall, managed four and was long-time owner of the Washington Senators. He was a force in major league baseball for more than 60 years.

Grimm, Charlie

(1925-36; 1932-38, 1944-49 and 1960, manager; 1939-42 and 1960, broadcaster)

Here's how much Charlie Grimm was a part of Cubs history: He played in Chicago with Grover Alexander, who started in the big leagues in 1911, and he managed Ron Santo and Billy Williams, whose careers lasted into the mid-1970s. A great-fielding first baseman, banjo-playing "Jolly Cholly" managed the Cubs to pennants in 1932 (he replaced Rogers Hornsby during the season), 1935 (a year in which the Cubs reeled off 21 consecutive wins) and 1945. He also was at the helm in 1938, another pennant-winning season, until giving way to Gabby Hartnett in July. His Cubs teams won 946 games. Grimm was a favorite of owner Phil Wrigley, who hired him three times as manager. When Grimm died, his widow scattered his ashes on Wrigley Field.

Hacker, Warren

(1948-56)

He, like many other Cubs starters of his era, teased the club with occasional success. In

1952, Warren Hacker won a career-best 15 games and was second in the N.L. in ERA with a mark of 2.58. He tossed five of his six career

shutouts in '52. Hacker was two outs from a no-hitter in 1955 when the Braves' George Crowe broke it up with a home run. He gave up lots of homers—in fact, a Cubs-record 38 that year.

Hands, Bill *(1966-72)*

"Froggy" was a tenacious competitor who came from the Giants in the same fortuitous deal that brought Randy Hundley. In 1969, Bill Hands personified the fire of the Cubs-Mets rivalry, getting into a season-long beanball war that at one point saw Tom Seaver fire a pitch into Hands' abdomen—after Hands had plunked the Mets' ace. As the Cubs sank in '69, Hands tried mightily to bail the boat, winning four of his last five decisions and finishing 20-14 with a 2.49 ERA. Hands threw 300 innings that season. He'd won 16 games the year before and he won 18 the next.

Hendley, Bob *(1965-67)*

On September 9, 1965, itinerant lefthander Bob Hendley, pitching for the Cubs, matched the great Sandy Koufax in a hitless battle until the Dodgers' Lou Johnson blooped a double with two out in the seventh inning. Los Angeles, which earlier had scored an unearned run without benefit of a hit, prevailed, 1-0, and Koufax got his fourth career no-hitter—a perfect game. Hendley, obtained earlier in the year from the Giants, got an "L" for his one-hitter. Epilogue: Five days later, Hendley beat Koufax, 2-1.

Herman, Billy *(1931-41)*

Second baseman Billy Herman teamed with shortstop Billy Jurges for seven-plus seasons as one of the best up-the-middle combinations in Cubs history. Herman's big-league career got off to a rough start—he was knocked unconscious in his first game when a foul ball caromed off his bat and struck him on the head. But Herman soon established himself as a hit-and-run master and standout fielder for Cubs teams that reached three World Series. He had three 200-hit seasons and batted .337 over one three-year stretch. Traded to Brooklyn in 1941, Herman had several more productive years and eventually made the Hall of Fame.

Hickman, Jim *(1968-73)*

People still talk about Pete Rose's aggressive play in the 12th inning of the 1970 All-Star Game, knocking over catcher Ray Fosse in a horrific collision while scoring the winning run. It was Jim Hickman's hit that brought Rose home. "Gentleman Jim" swung a productive bat for the 1969-72 Cubs. Said manager Leo Durocher in 1970: "Those fellas ought to kiss his feet. He carried us last year, and he's doing it again. We must be getting a little heavy for him." Hickman did some particularly heavy lifting in '70 with 32 homers and 115 RBIs.

Hobbie, Glen *(1957-64)*

A promising career seemed to loom when Glen Hobbie, at age 23, won 16 games for the Cubs in 1959. The righthander was perfect for 6⅔ innings in a game against St. Louis that year before Stan Musial rapped a double. Hobbie wound up with a one-hit, 1-0 victory. He posted 16 victories again in 1960 (while losing 20), but injuries, including a bad back, cut his career short.

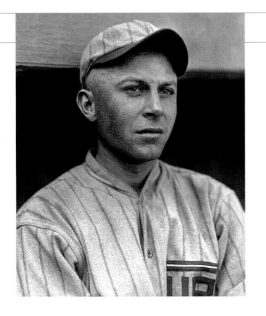

Hollocher, Charlie *(1918-24)*

A gifted hitter with a troubled life, Charlie Hollocher might have become one of baseball's greats. In 1922, he batted .340, with just five strikeouts, and led the league's shortstops in fielding and sensational plays. But Hollocher, who had left the team one year complaining of stomach pains and worked as a house painter, got sick again. He retired at age 28 with a .304 career average, still complaining of illness. He was a suicide at 44.

Holtzman, Ken *(1965-71, 1978-79)*

The memorable Ken Holtzman is the one who went 54-38 over a four-year stretch and pitched two no-hitters in his first stint with the Cubs, not the one who came back to finish his career after three World Series titles with Oakland and stints with the Orioles and Yankees. Holtzman twice won 17 games for the Cubs and went 9-0 in 1967, a year interrupted by military service. Despite his success, Holtzman was an irritant to management. He was the first Cub to bring an agent to salary negotiations; indignant G.M. John Holland threw the agent out of his office.

Hooton, Burt *(1971-75)*

He was an All-American pitcher at the University of Texas, a sensation in the minors (he struck out 19 in a Class AAA game) and an immediate success with the Cubs with his knuckle curve. As a late-season call-up in '71, Burt Hooton fanned 15 Mets. The next April, in his fourth big-league start, he no-hit the Phillies. But the Cubs gave up on him in 1975, trading him to Los Angeles for two young pitchers (who would win two games between them for Chicago). Hooton was a double-figure winner seven straight years for the Dodgers and appeared in three World Series.

Hornsby, Rogers

(1929-32; 1930-32, manager; 1958-59, coach)

The Cubs got him late in his Hall of Fame playing career, but he still had one spectacular year left in him. In 1929, Rogers Hornsby hit .380 and drove in 149 runs. The broken ankle that sidelined him most of the next season probably cost that powerful 1930 Cubs team a pennant. As a manager, Hornsby was less successful. "He was frank to the point of being cruel," wrote baseball historian Lee Allen, "and subtle as a belch." Hornsby wound up getting fired during the 1932 season—a year in which it was disclosed he'd borrowed money from his players to pay gambling debts. After the Cubs won the pennant, players didn't vote Hornsby one dime of their World Series money.

Hubbs, Ken *(1961-63)*

He was thought to have unlimited potential. In 1962, Ken Hubbs had broken major league records for consecutive errorless games (78) and chances (418) at second base, won the Gold Glove and been voted Rookie of the Year. He was athletic, polite, friendly, religious—and afraid of flying. He attacked that fear by getting a pilot's license after his rookie year. In 1964, just before spring training, Hubbs, 22, took off from Provo, Utah, with his best friend, bound for Colton, Calif., their hometown. Weather was poor, but Hubbs rejected suggestions that he postpone the trip. The plane crashed through the ice into Utah Lake, killing both men.

Hulbert, William

(owner, 1876-82)

Businessman William Hulbert ("I would rather be a lamp post in Chicago than a millionaire in any other city") was unhappy with the state of baseball in his town. Part owner of Chicago's National Association team, he got Albert Spalding, Cap Anson and others to defect from that league and started an essentially new team. Hulbert lined up support from three other Midwest cities and four in the East, and in February 1876 the National League—baseball's first recognized "major league"—was born. Hulbert and the league took special aim at curbing rowdyism, which had been so prevalent in the game.

Jackson, Randy *(1950-55, 1959)*

When Ernie Banks arrived as the Cubs short-stop, he shared the left side of the infield with "Handsome Ransom" Jackson. A pull hitter who stood close to the plate, Jackson packed some power—he once hit a ball onto the third floor of a building across Waveland Avenue. He played in the 1954 and 1955 All-Star Games, contributing a key hit in the N.L.'s comeback victory in '55. A baseball and football player for both TCU and Texas, Jackson was the only man to play in two consecutive Cotton Bowls with different schools.

Jackson, Larry
(1963-66)

Cocky, competitive Larry Jackson won 13 or more games a dozen years in a row while pitching for the Cardinals, Cubs and Phillies. He had by far his best season with the Cubs, compiling a 24-11 record for an eighth-place team in 1964. Jackson lost 21 the next year. The Cubs traded him to the Phillies just after the 1966 season began for two players they really wanted and a throw-in, an end-of-the-bullpen pitcher named Ferguson Jenkins.

Jones, Sam *(1955-56)*

Sam "Toothpick" Jones had a no-hitter going against the Pirates as the ninth inning opened on a May day at Wrigley in 1955. Jones walked the first three batters and was in danger of being lifted by manager Stan Hack. But the man with the extraordinary curveball struck out Dick Groat, Roberto Clemente and Frank Thomas to nail down the first Cubs no-hitter in 38 years and the first ever thrown in the majors by a black pitcher. Jones led the league in strikeouts that season with 198 but lost 20 games and set a 20th-century N.L. record with 185 walks. He was traded to the Cardinals in December 1956.

Jurges, Billy
(1931-38, 1946-47)

He was a fine-fielding fixture at shortstop in the '30s, paired with Billy Herman as the double-play duo on all three Cubs N.L. title teams of that decade. Billy Jurges also lived a story right out of the musical Chicago. In his Chicago hotel room in 1932, showgirl Violet Valli shot Jurges twice as they struggled over the .25 caliber handgun she'd threatened to use to kill herself. Jurges didn't press charges, and she wound up with a contract to sing and dance as Violet "I Did It for Love" Valli.

###

ⓀKawano, Yosh

(1943-present, equipment manager)

He was the "clubhouse boy" when he started, first with the minor league Los Angeles Angels in his hometown before moving to the big team. More than six decades later, into the Dusty Baker era, Yosh Kawano was still around, helping out in the visitors' locker room. His job description became more dignified—"equipment manager"—but whatever his title, Kawano has been a versatile employee. His extracurricular activities have included making bed checks on players, signing team autographed balls for derelict players and serving as a bench jockey.

Kelly, Mike "King" *(1880-86)*

His Hall of Fame plaque says his baserunning was "audacious," and that word summed up King Kelly. Mostly a right fielder and catcher, he played every position on the field, including pitcher. His popularity in Chicago was such that his picture poster was on the walls of barbershops and pool halls. He won two batting titles and once scored 155 runs in a season. Off the field—and occasionally on—he was notorious for his excesses. Asked if he drank, Kelly is said to have replied: "It depends on the length of the game." He died at 36 of pneumonia.

Kessinger, Don

(1964-75)

You say it "Kessinger'n'Beckert." Don Kessinger and Glenn Beckert were the double-play combination for the Leo Durocher Cubs—even though Durocher was not a Kessinger fan. Shortstop Kessinger didn't fit the manager's Gas House Gang mold—he didn't spit tobacco, swear, or drink, and he said "yes sir, no sir." But Durocher never found anyone better. Kessinger, a good glove man first, taught himself to switch hit in 1966 and became the Cubs' leadoff man, a player who could draw a walk and occasionally steal a base.

Kingman, Dave *(1978-80)*

When Dave Kingman joined the Cubs, he was playing for his fifth team in two seasons. He was noted for his prodigious home runs (three times he hit three in one game for the Cubs) and hostility to sportswriters (he threw a bucket of ice water on one in 1980 and said, "Now you've got something to write about for two days"). The media gave it back, calling him, among other things, childish, boorish and a jerk. In 1979, Kingman belted 48 homers for the Cubs—only three players have hit more in one season for the club (Sammy Sosa, Hack Wilson and Andre Dawson).

Kling, Johnny *(1900-08, 1910-11)*

He was a decent hitter and a good basestealer, but catcher Johnny Kling's biggest contribution was as a smart and skilled defensive player. The owner of a strong, accurate arm, he invented the snap throw from a catcher's crouch. The Cubs might have won five consecutive pennants if not for another skill of Kling's. In the offseason after the Cubs' 1908 World Series victory, their catcher won the world pocket billiards title. Unhappy about his salary, Kling quit baseball for billiards. The Cubs finished second in '09, then won another pennant when Kling rejoined the club the next year.

Lange, Bill *(1893-99)*

No one knows when "he can really go get 'em" was first applied to a center fielder, but it might well have been in the 1890s when Bill Lange ran down fly balls for Chicago with amazing skill and flair. Lange was equally flashy on the basepaths, stealing 65, 67, 84 and 73 bases in successive seasons. Oh, and he could hit, too, compiling a .330 average over seven years. The shortness of his career is a story in itself, albeit a disappointing one for Chicago. After the 1899 season, at age 28, Lange married into wealth and divorced himself from baseball.

INNING

Lee, Bill *(1934-43, 1947)*

No relation to the Bill Lee who, a generation later, would be called "Spaceman," the Cubs' guy was a big, quiet righthander who won 20 games for the pennant-winning team of 1935. He was even better when the Cubs ruled the N.L. again in '38: He led the league in wins (22), shutouts (nine) and ERA (2.66). In an 18-day span in September that year, he pitched four consecutive shutouts. Lee was a 19-game winner in 1939.

Leonard, Emil "Dutch"

(1949-53; coach, 1954-56)

In 1950, at age 41, Dutch Leonard became the Cubs' first full-time closer. A knuckleballer, he had been mostly a starter in a big-league career that began in 1933 and had won 20 games for the Senators in 1939. Leonard was a teammate of both Hack Wilson (1933-34, with Brooklyn) and Ernie Banks (1953, Cubs).

Lieber, Jon

(1999-2002)

In five years with the Pirates, big righthander Jon Lieber won as many as 11 games just once, so perhaps it's understandable that Pittsburgh shipped him to the Cubs for Brant Brown. Once in Chicago, Lieber was a steady starter. He won 10, 12 and then 20 games, using unspectacular pitches but making the most of excellent control. In 2002, he was averaging not even one walk per game when his arm gave out in midseason. After undergoing Tommy John surgery and then becoming a free agent, he came back in 2004 with the Yankees.

Long, Dale *(1957-59)*

A short-term Chicago first baseman who played mostly other places, Dale Long is unforgettable for two reasons:
1. As a Pirate, the year before he came to the Cubs, he set a record by hitting home runs in eight consecutive games.
2. As a Cub, he became the first left-handed catcher in the majors in 56 years, getting behind the plate in two games.

Madlock, Bill *(1974-76)*

The Cubs have tried countless third basemen since Ron Santo departed after the 1973 season, and Bill Madlock was the first. Obtained in a trade that sent Ferguson Jenkins to the Rangers, Madlock rewarded management by becoming the only 20th-century Cub to win two straight batting titles. "Mad Dog" then asked for a salary he thought commensurate with that distinction. Said owner Phil Wrigley: "We'll trade Madlock if another team is foolish enough to have him." It wasn't a hard sell. Bill Madlock played 11 more years for four other clubs and finished with two more batting crowns.

Malone, Pat *(1928-34)*

Like Hack Wilson, pitcher Pat Malone was a tough kid from Pennsylvania. The two were drinking buddies and

brawlers—hecklers called Wilson and Malone "Whiskey Head and Beer Belly." Malone pitched in the minors for seven years, kept there more by his off-field habits than any shortcomings as a pitcher, until manager Joe McCarthy acquired him from the Giants' organization. Malone lost his first five decisions as a Cub, but McCarthy stuck with him. He wound up with 18 wins as a rookie, 22 for the pennant-winning Cubs of 1929 and 20 for the 1930 club.

Matthews, Gary

(1984-87; coach, 2003-present)

Wrote one sportswriter: "Why is it a player who gives so much of himself is traded so often?" After more than a decade of strong hitting, good baserunning, solid outfield play and hustle, Gary Matthews found himself with his fourth team, the Cubs, in 1984. Matthews' age (34) was no doubt a reason. But G.M. Dallas Green was betting "Sarge" had one more good year left—and he did. After a poor '83 season with the Phillies, Matthews hit .291 with 82 RBIs for the division-winning 1984 Cubs. Two decades later, he was still a Wrigley Field presence as the Cubs' hitting coach and then first base coach.

Matthews, Wid *(1950-56, general manager)*

The Cubs wound up in seventh place the year Wid Matthews was hired as G.M. They finished last the year he was fired. In between, Matthews (a) let his old boss, Branch Rickey, snooker him into trading Andy Pafko to the Dodgers; (b) predicted catcher Harry Chiti would be "the new Gabby Hartnett," and (c) told the press before the 1956 season that he expected the Cubs to "crash into the first division." Pafko helped Brooklyn reach one World Series and played in two Series with Milwaukee; Chiti flopped, and the Cubs made the first division in ... 1967.

McCarthy, Joe

(1926-30, manager)

The Cubs hired Joe McCarthy after finishing last in 1925. McCarthy, who had been managing Louisville of the American Association, pushed the Cubs to draft Hack Wilson from the Giants' system, got Riggs Stephenson and Pat Malone from the minors, chased off Grover Alexander and his drinking habit, obtained Kiki Cuyler from Pittsburgh and then dealt for Rogers Hornsby. In five years, he produced one pennant and five first-division finishes. But the Cubs, after losing the World Series in 1929 and falling just short of a pennant in 1930, let McCarthy go. "Marse Joe" then led the Yankees to seven Series titles.

McLish, Cal *(1949, 1951)*

He won five games total for two last-place Cubs teams. In Cubs lore, he is unforgettable in name only. That name: Calvin Coolidge Julius Caesar Tuskahoma McLish. "My parents had six kids before me, and my dad didn't get to name any of them," McLish explained. "When I came along, he tried to catch up." Late in his career, McLish found success—he had 16-8 and 19-8 seasons for Cleveland and an 11-5 year with the Phillies.

Merkle, Fred *(1917-20)*

He's important not for what he did for the Cubs in their uniform, but for what he did for them as a Giant in 1908. Fred Merkle, a 19-year-old substitute that day, failed to touch second base as the Giants scored the apparent winning run in the ninth inning of a late-season game with Chicago at the Polo Grounds. After the melee that ensued, the game ended in a tie. When the regular-season schedule ended two weeks later, the Cubs and Giants were deadlocked for first place at 98-55, necessitating a makeup of the tie game. The Cubs won, 4-2, and went on to win their second and last World Series title. Years later, Merkle was the Cubs' regular first baseman.

Meyer, Russ *(1946-48, 1956)*

More than one former Cubs team-mate has told this story: Russ Meyer got into a barroom argument with

an ex-girl-friend. They got loud and face to face. And then she bit off a piece of his nose. "The Mad Monk" was a screw-ball pitcher in both sens-es. He won 10 games in his first full year as a Chicago starter, but the Cubs were uncomfortable with his hot temper and sold him to the Phillies. He had big years with the Phils (17-8) and Dodgers (15-5) before pitching (poor-ly) for the Cubs again in 1956.

Mieske, Matt
(1998)

Ninety years after the Cubs beat the Giants in a makeup game to get to the World Series, they met the Giants in a play-off game to decide the N.L. wild card. The Cubs won again. The unlikeli-est of heroes was Matt Mieske, a spare outfield-er who, entering the extra game, had 28 hits all season—the part of the season he didn't play in the minors. Mieske's two-run, bases-loaded pinch single pro-vided the eventual mar-gin in the 5-3 victory that thrust the Cubs into the postseason.

Miller, Hack *(1922-25)*

His strength was legendary. Lawrence "Hack" Miller uprooted trees at Catalina Island, where the Cubs trained. He picked

up cars by their bumpers, bent iron bars with his hands, pounded spikes into wood with his fist. As for his baseball skills, Miller hit .352 as a 28-year-old Cubs rookie in 1922, contributing two three-run homers in the 26-23 win over the Phillies that still stands as the record for the most total runs scored in a big-league game. Slow and a liability in the outfield, he soon flamed out.

Monday, Rick *(1972-76)*

In April 1976, Rick Monday was in center field for the Cubs when two people ran onto the field at Dodger Stadium and tried to set an American flag on fire. Monday charged over and scooped up the flag on the run. "If you're going to burn the flag," he said later, "don't do it in front of me. I've been to too many veterans hospitals and seen too many broken bodies of guys who tried to protect it." Aside from those heroics, Monday hit a career-high 32 homers in '76 and batted .270 over his five years as a Cub.

Moreland, Keith
(1982-87)

You could say Keith Moreland was versatile. One writer put it another way: "The guy can hit, but where to hide him?" Moreland played the outfield, third base and first base for the Cubs, and did a little catching. And he hit. He rolled up a couple of .300-plus years in Chicago and was a consistent run-producer. On the almost-pennant '84 team, he shared the outfield with two other of Dallas Green's ex-Phillies, Bob Dernier and Gary Matthews, and drove in 80 runs. The next year, he had 106 RBIs.

Moryn, Walt *(1956-60)*

He was a long-ball hitter, with 23- and 26-homer seasons (and a three-homer game) as a Cub. Yet the enduring image of Walt Moryn is with his glove. It was May 15, 1960, and Don Cardwell, obtained by the Cubs in a trade two days earlier, had a no-hitter going at Wrigley with two out in the ninth. The Cardinals' Joe Cunningham hit a hump-backed line drive to left. "Moose" Moryn, not noted for his grace in the outfield, charged in, reached down and caught the ball at shoelace level.

Myers, Randy
(1993-95)

A tale of the hired gun: He arrived as a free agent, and he left as one three seasons later, but in between Randy Myers defined the Cubs' bullpen. His first year, the left-hander broke the N.L. record for saves with 53 (a figure that remains the Cubs' record). His total of 112 in just three seasons trails only Lee Smith and Bruce Sutter in franchise career saves. The downside: In the winter of 1992-93, the Cubs told staff ace Greg Maddux they couldn't meet his asking price because they'd set aside money to hire, among others, Myers.

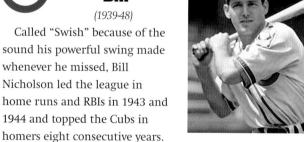

Nicholson, Bill
(1939-48)

Called "Swish" because of the sound his powerful swing made whenever he missed, Bill Nicholson led the league in home runs and RBIs in 1943 and 1944 and topped the Cubs in homers eight consecutive years. In the second game of a doubleheader at the Polo Grounds in '44, Nicholson was walked intentionally with the bases loaded—he had homered three times in the first game and once in the nightcap. He suffered from diabetes, which eventually affected his eyesight. The first sign may have been in the Cubs' pennant year of 1945, when his hitting fell off precipitously.

Novikoff, Lou
(1941-44)

He was known as a great minor league slugger. It turned out he was a great major league flake. "The Mad Russian," Lou Novikoff, developed a fear of Wrigley Field's vines, and thus, reasonably, avoided catching many fly balls that came down near the ivy. Making matters worse, he was a notoriously poor outfielder in the first place. In his spare time, Novikoff played a harmonica with considerable skill and fed his Russian wolfhound caviar; in his work time, he put up a .300 batting average in the only season in which he was a regular for the Cubs.

Pafko, Andy *(1943-51)*

He came out of small-town Wisconsin and won lasting affection in the big city. A mainstay of the last pennant-winning Cubs team in 1945, Andy Pafko had great range in center field and a steady bat. In 1950, he hit 36 homers while striking out just 32 times. Cubs fans of a certain age still remember the four-for-four trade in 1951 that sent popular "Handy Andy" to Brooklyn: Each team moved an outfielder, an infielder, a catcher and a pitcher to the other. In the end, the only player who mattered was Pafko, who had a 30-homer season in '51 and played in the majors through 1959.

Overall, Orval

(1906-10, 1913)

As would be the case in 1945 and 1984, the Cubs went pitcher-shopping in midseason 1906. They got Orval Overall, a big righthander, from Cincinnati for $2,000 and a marginal pitcher. Overall went 12-3 the rest of the season as the Cubs won their first of three consecutive pennants. With his great curveball, he got even better. In 1907, Overall threw eight shutouts. In 1909, he struck out 205 batters, a total not exceeded by a Cub until Ferguson Jenkins fanned 236 in 1967, and tossed nine shutouts. In the only two World Series the Cubs have ever won, he was 3-0 with an ERA of 0.99.

Pappas, Milt *(1970-73)*

Furious after pitching a no-hitter? That was Milt Pappas. He was one strike from a perfect game on September 2, 1972, at Wrigley Field when he walked Padres pinch hitter Larry Stahl on a 3-2 pitch. Screaming mad over umpire Bruce Froemming's call, Pappas then retired the next batter on a pop fly. Pappas wasn't known for a sweet disposition. Players said he and Joe Pepitone were at the center of a heated clubhouse meeting with manager Leo Durocher that led to Durocher's departure and the breakup of the core of the so-close '69 team. Pappas twice won 17 games as a Cub.

Pepitone, Joe *(1970-73)*

He made his name and his bright-lights reputation with the Yankees, and didn't tone it down much when he came to Chicago. The Cubs weren't accustomed to his style, which included long hair and longer nights on the town. Pepitone sometimes showed up for games on a motorcycle, and bought into a bar on Rush Street. And, oh yeah, he played baseball—first base, where he was excellent, and the outfield—and hit over .300 in his only close-to-full season with the Cubs.

Pieper, Pat

(1916-74, public address announcer)

"Attention, attention please. Have your pencils and scorecards ready. ..." For nearly six decades, anyone who attended a game at Wrigley Field heard that call, followed immediately by the

starting lineups, followed a few minutes later with "Play baaaaalll-ll!" That was Pat Pieper, the Cubs' public address announcer. Perhaps no one has seen so much baseball history up close.

And close he was. Until management, worried about his advancing age, moved him to the press box, Pieper sat on the field behind home plate. In the early days, he called out the players' names through a bullhorn.

Prior, Mark *(2002-present)*

Some have arrived in the big leagues with similar fanfare and expectations. Few have delivered so quickly and decisively as Mark Prior. A standout at Southern Cal, he was the second overall pick in the 2001 draft. The righthander blew through the minor leagues and made the big club early in 2002, at age 21, amazing people with his poise and control. He won 18 games in his first full season, 2003, as the Cubs reached the League Championship Series. Injuries shortened his first and third seasons. An all-time great? An all-time heartbreak? A clutch—but in vain—16-strikeout performance in the last week of the 2004 season gave hope of the former.

Quinlan, Jack

(1956-64, broadcaster)

Years later, Vince Lloyd said the man he succeeded as the Cubs' radio play-by-play man, Jack Quinlan, had "the best broadcasting voice I ever heard." Quinlan's customary opening, "The Chicago Cubs are on the air," carried the enthusiasm that paired with humor to characterize his style. Quinlan was killed in an auto wreck in Arizona as spring training was beginning in 1965. It was the winter after the Cubs had lost young second baseman Ken Hubbs in a plane crash.

Ramirez, Aramis

(2003-present)

That revolving door at third base since Ron Santo departed is revolving no more (if such can be said in this era of player movement). Obtained from Pittsburgh in July 2003, Aramis Ramirez gave the appearance of lending stability at the hot corner. Of course, such appearances have been deceiving for the Cubs for three decades. But in 2004 Ramirez broke Santo's club record for homers at the position (33, set in 1965) by hitting 36 and joined Santo and Andy Pafko as the only Cubs third basemen to reach 100 RBIs in a season. More good news: Even as a 10-year pro by season's end, Ramirez was only 26 years old.

Reagan, Ronald

(1933-36, broadcaster)

As he re-created play-by-play of a Cubs game from telegraphic dispatches, the wire went dead. So announcer Ronald Reagan, based in Des Moines, had Augie Galan foul off pitch after pitch after pitch. After his radio days, Reagan reportedly went into acting and politics, two other professions in which people sometimes make up stuff.

Regan, Phil

(1968-72; 1997-98, coach)

Sandy Koufax gave "The Vulture" his nickname after Phil Regan, in his pre-Cubs days, picked up two wins in one week in relief of brilliant Koufax starts. Regan's time as the Cubs' top bullpen man coincided with the team's pennant-challenging years. He threw a slider and a spitball—or so it appeared. Suspicion that Regan illegally wet the ball with spit, grease or something else was ongoing. In one game in 1968, umpire Chris Pelekoudas twice gave Cincinnati batters do-overs, contending that Regan had retired them on spitballs.

Reuschel, Rick *(1972-81, 1983-84)*

"They're good pitchers," says one of the characters in the play Bleacher Bums, "but they're built like turnips." The reference was to the beefy Reuschels—Rick (135 Cubs victories) and older brother Paul (a mere 12). After Ferguson Jenkins left, Rick was the Cubs' best pitcher of the '70s, posting double-figure win totals in nine consecutive seasons overall. In 1977, with the help of ace reliever Bruce Sutter, he got off to a 15-3 start. Sutter got hurt and the Cubs' big lead in the N.L. East unraveled, but Reuschel wound up 20-10. Only Jenkins has started more Cubs games than Rick Reuschel.

Rhodes, Karl "Tuffy"
(1993-95)

Dwight Gooden was, to be sure, in decline by opening day, 1994. Tuffy Rhodes was, well, Tuffy Rhodes, a player who had totaled five home runs in four years of scuffling around the fringes of the National

League. Remarkably, Rhodes hit three homers off Gooden that day at Wrigley Field—but the Cubs lost to the Mets, anyway. Rhodes hit five more home runs in the majors, then, say-

onara. In Japan, he proved he really could hit the long ball, tying Sadaharu Oh's single-season record with 55 homers.

Rush, Bob *(1948-57)*

Big, easy-going Bob Rush was the No. 1 starter on Cubs teams that didn't have many No. 1 days. He was a double-figure winner seven times for Chicago. In 1952, Rush pitched three consecutive shutouts in one stretch and finished with a 17-13 record and a 2.70 ERA. Of his losses, two were 1-0 and one was 2-0. He was the winning pitcher in the '52 All-Star Game, with the winning blow a Hank Sauer home run. Rush won 110 games in his 10 years as a Cub.

Ryan, Jimmy *(1885-89, 1891-1900)*

This hell-raiser once helped toss a keg of beer out a hotel window, narrowly missing manager Cap Anson. Jimmy Ryan was an outfielder who caught the tail end of the Cubs' first dominant era and missed the second, but he played 14 seasons for Chicago and hit .300 nine times. He's the only Cub who has hit for the cycle twice, and he fell one homer short of being the first man in a Cubs uniform with at least 100 homers, 2,000 hits and a .300 career average. That honor was left for Mark Grace.

Ⓢ

Schulte, Frank "Wildfire"

(1904-16)

He was the strong-hitting right fielder on the Cubs' only two World Series champions. In the 1908 Series, he batted .389. He was the first major leaguer with 20 or more doubles, triples, home runs and steals in one season. No one accomplished the feat again until Willie Mays. Wildfire Schulte tied for the N.L. homer lead in 1910 and topped the league in 1911 with the impressive total of 21. The Cubs' all-time leader in steals of home with 22, Schulte broke in with the club in 1904 and was still around when the team moved into the ballpark at Clark and Addison in 1916.

Smalley, Roy

(1948-53)

George Will: "From Roy Smalley I learned the truth about the word 'overdue.' Smalley retired after 11 seasons with a lifetime batting average of .227. He was still overdue." A not-very-good shortstop who was a not-very-good hitter, Smalley led the majors in errors (an astonishing 51) and strikeouts (114) in the same season (1950). He was a symbol of Cubs futility in the late '40s and early '50s—one gag was that the Cubs' double-play combination was (second baseman Eddie) Miksis to Smalley to the dugout. His replacement at shortstop for the Cubs: a fellow named Ernie Banks.

Selma, Dick *(1969)*

Walking from the clubhouse to the dugout during an early-season game in 1969, pitcher Dick Selma spontaneously urged Wrigley's bleacher fans to start yelling, and waved his arms. Minutes later, Ernie Banks hit a home run, and a tradition was born. Selma, when he wasn't pitching that year, stationed himself in the bullpen, waved a hanky and exhorted the bleacher crowd, whose members soon outfitted themselves in yellow helmets. For the one season (10-8 record) they got out of Selma, the Cubs traded Joe Niekro, who wound up with 221 career victories (24 as a Cub).

Sianis, William *(1945, fan)*

One of these centuries, when the Cubs win another World Series, this story will be forgotten. Until then ... William Sianis was owner of the Billy Goat Tavern, a dank place that still operates in subterranean Chicago. In 1945, he was denied the use of his box-seat ticket for Game 4 of the Series because he wanted his pet goat to accompany him. After Wrigley Field police escorted Sianis and his smelly pet out, Sianis put a curse on the Cubs, who haven't won a pennant since. Yes, his curse still has their goat. (William's nephew Sam, above, brought a goat to Wrigley in 2003 in an effort to end the hex. Alas, no luck.)

Spalding, Albert *(1876-78; 1876-77, manager; 1882-92, owner)*

Albert Spalding's Hall of Fame plaque calls him an "organizational genius." He inspired the National League's creation by defecting from Boston (National Association) with his best teammates and pushing William Hulbert to form a great Chicago team and a league to house it. He called baseball "the national pastime" and promoted it through his Spalding Guide annuals. He also profited from the game through the sporting goods firm bearing his name, becoming the exclusive supplier of N.L. baseballs. He pitched the first game in the Chicago franchise's history, winning at Louisville, 4-0, on April 25, 1876, and managed the club in its first two seasons.

Speake, Bob

(1955, 1957)

The Cubs got off to a hot start in 1955. The reasons, said manager Stan Hack: "Pitching and Bob Speake." Speake, a 24-year-old rookie outfielder/first baseman, was a sensation in May, hitting 10 home runs and driving in 25 runs over a 20-game stretch. Alas, he finished the season with only 12 homers and 43 RBIs. He hit 16 homers in 129 games in 1957. His batting average in 224 games as a Cub: .227.

Steinfeldt, Harry

(1906-10)

As the third baseman in the famed Tinker-Evers-Chance championship infields, he's the answer to one of baseball's favorite trivia questions. Here's a harder one: Who played the position with Joe, Johnny and Frank before Harry Steinfeldt came along in 1906? Answer: James "Doc" Casey. After eight nondescript years with Cincinnati, Steinfeldt became an immediate hit with the Cubs, topping the league in hits and fielding average in his first year and sharing the lead in RBIs.

Stephenson, Riggs *(1926-34)*

Joe McCarthy pulled off several coups as Cubs manager. One was finding a major league talent, Riggs Stephenson, on a minor league roster. Stephenson, who had been a standout hitter as a utilityman for Cleveland before the Indians lost interest, played left field for the Cubs. "Old Hoss," a former Alabama fullback, was slow and had no arm, but, oh, could he hit. He racked up eight consecutive .315-plus seasons—including back-to-back .362 and .367 marks. Stephenson's .336 is still the highest career average as a Cub (tied by Bill Madlock, who played only three years in Chicago).

Stone, Steve

(1974-76; 1983-2000 and 2003-04, broadcaster)

He had several good years as a pitcher, and one super season—he won the Cy Young Award after winning 25 games for Baltimore in 1980. That was well after

three so-so years (23-20 record) as a Cub. Steve Stone was the key man the Cubs got from the White Sox when they traded Wrigley Field icon Ron Santo across town. Three years later, he became the first Cub to walk away as a free agent. Stone stood out more in the booth at Wrigley than he ever did on the mound. He drew more attention than he wanted in 2004, though, his criticism of an underachieving Cubs team stirring controversy between the TV analyst and those in uniform. He decided to resign 3½ weeks after the season ended.

Sunday, Billy *(1883-87)*

"Chicago, Chicago ... the town that Billy Sunday could not shut down." He never hit .300 as a fleet, part-time outfielder, and his fielding average in his last Chicago

season was .766, but he's immortalized in song for his later, longer career as an evangelist and temperance advocate: "Whiskey is all right in its place—but its place is hell." Sunday's hard-drinking teammates gave him plenty of evidence of the effects of alcohol, and he changed his life one night when he heard revival hymns outside a tavern where he sat with Mike Kelly.

Sutcliffe, Rick *(1984-91)*

He had a fine, long career, yet is best known for one stretch of excellence. Rick Sutcliffe rolled up an other-worldly 16-1 record in 3½ months after the Cubs acquired him from Cleveland for Joe Carter and Mel Hall in June 1984, the year that was magic until the Padres did their trick. He captured the Cy Young Award, then won 66 more games for the Cubs, including 16 for the '89 division champions. His 6-7 frame, red beard and stern stare were an intimidating sight and much at odds with the cheerful face he presented later as a network television analyst.

Tapani, Kevin

(1997-2001)

He was 33 years old, with nearly a decade in the majors, by the time he got to the Cubs, but Kevin Tapani saved his best season for Chicago. He had a 19-9 record for the 1998 Cubs despite a 4.85 ERA. In the Division Series, he fell victim to the hitting breakdown that led to the Cubs' elimination in three games by the Braves. He shut out Atlanta for eight innings in Game 2, but Javy Lopez homered in the ninth and the Cubs lost, 2-1, in 10 innings.

Tappe, Elvin

(1954-56, 1958, 1960, 1962; manager, 1961-62; coach, 1959-65)

"The College of Coaches concept," Elvin Tappe said in 1961, "is the best thing that has happened to baseball since the spitball." It was Tappe who, as a coach, planted the idea with owner Phil Wrigley. By all accounts, Tappe hadn't envisioned floating coaches alternating as manager. The former Cubs reserve catcher thought the team should have a set group of coaches who would teach the "Cubs way" at all levels and not turn over with every managerial change. Wrigley took it to the next level, with rotating managers, including Tappe twice. The great scheme didn't work.

Tinker, Joe

(1902-12, 1916; manager, 1916)

"Tinker to Evers to Chance" formed in 1902. Joe Tinker at shortstop came first, taking over the position on opening day. Frank Chance later switched from second-string catcher to first base, and Johnny Evers arrived in September to play between them. Tinker remained the Cubs' shortstop for 11 years. He was traded at his request after Evers, with whom he feuded, was named manager for 1913, then returned as manager himself in 1916. Tinker led the league in fielding at his position five times.

Veeck, Bill

(1933-41, front office)

When his father, the general manager, died, Bill Veeck went to work in the Cubs' front office. He never got his dad's old job, but Veeck went on to fame for the good (bringing the first black player to the American League), the bad (he owned the St. Louis Browns) and the funny (the midget he hired to pinch hit). It was budding promoter Veeck who was responsible for installing the Wrigley Field ivy. And it was Veeck who unsuccessfully lobbied owner Phil Wrigley to put lights in Wrigley Field, more than a half century before it happened.

Veeck, William

(1919-33, general manager)

As would be the case a generation later, a Cubs owner hired a baseball writer to run his team. William Veeck Sr. even came from the same

newspaper as '40s G.M. Jim Gallagher. He and his boss, owner William Wrigley Jr., shared some characteristics: The two didn't know a lot about baseball, but they were imaginative promoters. They initiated regular broadcasts of Cubs games and made ladies days popular. Veeck also had the distinction of finding Joe McCarthy in the minors to manage his team—and then firing him after five seasons.

Verban, Emil *(1948-50)*

This infielder became the namesake for a society of mostly D.C.-based Cubs fans including Ronald Reagan, Dick Cheney and Hillary Clinton. He was not amused, especially when word got around that his name was chosen to symbolize Cubs mediocrity. The fact is, Emil Verban hit .280 as a Cub (and .272 overall in the majors), struck out just 74 times in 2,911 big-league at-bats and was a starter on a World Series champion (1944 Cardinals).

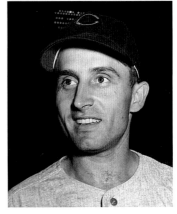

Waitkus, Eddie

(1941, 1946-48)

Nineteen-year-old Ruth Ann Steinhagen was obsessed, with a ballplayer she'd never met. He was Eddie Waitkus, a first baseman the Cubs had traded to Philadelphia after the 1948 season. When the Phillies came to Chicago the next June, she checked into their hotel and sent Waitkus a message to come to her room about "something important." When he arrived, she shot him in the chest. He recovered and played until the mid-1950s. She went to a mental institution. A Waitkus-like shooting became a key scene in Bernard Malamud's novel, The Natural, and the Robert Redford movie that followed.

Wallis, Joe *(1975-78)*

"Tarzan" Wallis, diver and outfielder, was Joe Pepitone's successor as good Cubs copy—but without Joe's skills. "We should have a few more of that kind of character," Jack Brickhouse said of Wallis. "There are too many ballplayers reading The Wall Street Journal nowadays." A two-triple game not long after his major league debut offered hope that he was a star of the future, but that star was already pretty dim when he broke his leg trying an Evel Knievel-style motorcycle stunt.

Walton, Jerome *(1989-92)*

What a way to break into the majors. Center fielder Jerome Walton hit in 30 consecutive games in 1989, the longest Cubs batting streak of the 20th century, and was voted N.L. Rookie of the Year after finishing with a .293 average and 24 stolen bases. Then, poof! His average plummeted—all the way to .127 over 55 at-bats in 1992. Second in the '89 N.L. rookie voting: fellow Cubs outfielder Dwight Smith.

Warneke, Lon

(1930-36, 1942-43, 1945)

"The Arkansas Hummingbird," master of a big-breaking curveball, was the Cubs' best pitcher on the successful teams of the early 1930s. With the '32 pennant winner, he led the National League with 22 wins and a 2.37 ERA, and he got the Cubs' only two victories in the '35 Series. After he finished pitching—he was a 20-game winner three times overall—Lon Warneke became an N.L. umpire and served in that capacity from 1949 through 1955.

Weeghman, Charles

(owner, 1916-21)

Owner of a restaurant chain and the short-lived Chicago Whales of the Federal League, he's the man who put a ballpark in the area bounded by Clark and Addison streets and Waveland and Sheffield avenues. When the Federal League folded, Charlie

Weeghman led a 10-man syndicate that bought the Cubs in 1916. Three years later, William Wrigley purchased controlling interest of the team, and the park became Wrigley Field in late 1926.

Whitlow, Bob

(1963-64, athletic director)

On top of the College of Coaches, Phil Wrigley installed retired Air Force Col. Robert V. Whitlow as "athletic director." Said Whitlow, who in spring training in 1963 lined up bemused Cubs players and led them in calisthenics: "Analyzing our team on paper, I say it is possible for us to take all the marbles." Six N.L. teams wound up with more marbles in '63, seven the next year. When Whitlow quit, Wrigley weighed in: "Baseball simply refused to accept his ideas. He was too far ahead of his time."

Williams, Mitch *(1989-90)*

His first save for the Cubs was, fittingly, a wild one. Opening day, 1989, ninth inning. Mitch Williams allows three singles, loading the bases for the Phillies, then strikes out the side (Mike Schmidt included). His line: 1⅔ innings, two walks, a balk, three strikeouts, no runs. "I pitch like my hair is on fire," he once said. The lefthander's two seasons as a Cub netted 52 saves. With almost as many walks as strikeouts, he left millions of fans with gnawed fingernails. To get the "Wild Thing," the Cubs had traded Rafael Palmeiro and Jamie Moyer to Texas in a nine-player swap.

Williamson, Ned *(1879-89)*

Chicago third baseman Ned Williamson held the majors' single-season home run record, with 27, longer than Babe Ruth held his at 60. There's a catch, though. He hit the 27 in 1884. That year, fly balls hit over the right field fence, less than 200 feet from home plate at Lakefront Park, counted as homers; previously, they'd been doubles. Williamson, a righthanded hitter, adjusted his swing to take advantage. The following year, the team moved to West Side Park. Williamson never hit as many as 10 homers in a season before or after '84.

Wilson, Bert

(1944-55, broadcaster)

As the radio voice for Cubs baseball, Bert Wilson was Cubs first, baseball second. Listeners could count on him saying, "I don't care who wins, as long as it's the Cubs," and, with the Cubs behind, "The game is never over until the last man is out."

Wood, Kerry *(1998, 2000-present)*

A Hall of Fame-bound burly righthander from Texas with a talented and durable arm has twice struck out 20 batters in a game. His name is Roger Clemens. Another burly righthander from Texas, this one with a talented and fragile arm, also has a 20-strikeout game. His name is Kerry Wood. Making just his fifth major league start at age 20, the Cubs' Wood gave up one scratch hit, walked no one and fanned 20 Astros on May 6, 1998. He went on to fashion a 13-6 record as a rookie, striking out 233 batters in 166⅔ innings. Eleven months after his milestone game, Wood had elbow ligament surgery. He missed all of 1999. There have been injury scares since. But when healthy, Wood still dazzles, striking out more than one an inning, giving up far less than a hit an inning.

Wrigley, Phil *(1932-77, owner)*

"Beautiful Wrigley Field" isn't just an advertising slogan. It's a symbol of Philip K. Wrigley's way of running the Cubs. Never a baseball fan, Wrigley inherited the team from his father, who

made it the son's responsibility to keep it going as a civic endeavor. He didn't go to games, didn't make speeches, didn't make waves. He forbade lights at his field out of concern for the neighborhood. Wrigley, owner of a huge, rich corporation, didn't have nearly such success in baseball. Just before his death, he declared, "I have outlived my usefulness. Everything has changed."

Wyse, Hank *(1942-47)*

The addition of Hank Borowy was credited with putting the Cubs over the top in 1945, but the leader of the pitching staff that year was Hank Wyse, a tough oil-field worker who posted 22 victories and pitched 23 complete games. What's more, he matched that year's 2.68 ERA the next season, when the National League's good hitters were back from the war.

Wrigley, William Jr.

(1921-32, owner)

He began by selling retailers the soap his father manufactured in Philadelphia. He came up with the idea of giving his customers baking soda as an incentive. When that proved popular, he sold the baking soda, and his new incentive was chewing gum. By 1891, he was in Chicago, manufacturing the gum at William Wrigley Jr. Co. He invested $50,000 when Charles Weeghman bought the Chicago National League baseball team in 1916. In three years, he bought controlling interest, and by 1921 he was the sole owner. He died at 70 without fulfilling his wish for a World Series championship. No one could have imagined how long it would be.

Zabel, Zip *(1913-15)*

George Washington Zabel won 12 games as an unremarkable major league pitcher, but he lives in Cubs history for a performance against Brooklyn. On a June day in 1915, Zabel came on to pitch with two out in the first inning. He worked the rest of the game—a major league relief record of $18\frac{1}{3}$ innings—and allowed two runs, nine hits and one walk. The Cubs and Zabel won, 4-3.

Young, Don *(1965, 1969)*

He is remembered for a very bad inning in the outfield, but Don Young did not cost the 1969 Cubs the pennant. Young misplayed two fly balls in the ninth inning of a game at New York. A 3-1 Cubs lead became, first, a 4-3 loss, then a clubhouse controversy when manager Leo Durocher and team captain Ron Santo harshly criticized Young in front of sportswriters. That was the day, the story goes, that momentum found the '69 Miracle Mets. Some facts: The game was July 8. The Cubs started the day in first place, five games ahead of the Mets, and they finished July six games in front.

Zambrano, Carlos

(2001-present)

He was plenty good as a 22-year-old in 2003, winning 13 games and fashioning a 3.11 earned-run average. With certain Hall of Famer Greg Maddux rejoining the Cubs' staff in 2004 and Mark Prior and Kerry Wood primed to replicate their heroics of the previous season, Carlos Zambrano needed to be plenty good again to receive his due. He was, and he did. Often as dominant as he was excitable, and pitching as though he were the Cubs' ace, Zambrano compiled a 16-8 record in '04 and put together a 2.75 ERA.

Zimmerman, Heinie

(1907-16)

He was the only Cub to win a Triple Crown—or not. Revisionist statistics-keeping for 1912 has reduced the RBI part of what the record long showed as a .372-14-103 season (and stripped him, in some quarters, of the milestone hitting feat). Other contradictions abound. Heinie Zimmerman was the Cubs' best hitter for most of a decade, but an ineffectual infielder and trouble otherwise. He was once ejected from three games in five days, once beaten up by manager Frank Chance after challenging him and once accused of throwing ammonia on a teammate. After his Chicago days, he was banned from baseball in a betting scandal.

Zimmer, Don

(1960-61; coach, 1984-86; manager, 1988-91)

The man with the face that Joe Garagiola likened to a blocked punt spent only a small part of his 5½ decades in baseball with the Cubs. But Don Zimmer endeared himself to Chicago by presiding over 1989's "Boys of Zimmer." With essentially the same cast as the year before, the Cubs improved by 16 games and won the N.L. East.

14 BARTMAN GAME

15

INNING 7

Ten Most Memorable

SENSATIONAL FINISH IN NAT[?] LEAGUE.

Chicago, New York and Pittsburg for Honors Until Last Week[?] Season.

CHICAGO TEAM OF 1908.

1) Kieh, (2) Trainer Slmmons, (3) Kling, (4) Reulbach, (5) Zimmerman, (6) Marshall, (7) Schulte, (8) Pfeister, (9) Frazer, (10) Lundgren, (11) Hofman, (12) Manager Chance, (13) Overall, (14) Brown, (19) Evers, (20) Sheckard, (21) Durbin, (22) Steale, [?]

FINAL GAME OF WORLD'S SERIES OF 1908.—AT DETROIT.

CUB 0808 24 6 105 A 10.50
10.50 GATE F CLUB
24
CA 6K
6 105
CUB 1244
A12MAY8

TURNING ON THE LIGHTS
AUGUST 8 1988

DURHAM'S MISPLAY

FLY-BALL PHOBIA

1929, 1969, 1998

September 28, 1938

Hartnett's Homer

Moments

Ruth's called shot -- 1932

September 23, 1908 -- Merkle's Blunder

INNING

MOMENT

①

Hartnett's Homer in the Gloamin'
1938

Gabby Hartnett's dramatic home run did not actually put the Cubs in the 1938 World Series. But it is the closest thing in team history to Bobby Thomson's famed "The Giants win the pennant!" moment. Under Hartnett, who became playing manager in July, the Cubs first slumped—

Brown

they were in fourth place and nine games out on August 20. They still trailed by 1½ games as Pittsburgh came to Chicago for a showdown series in the last week of the season. The Cubs won the opener, 2-1, behind Dizzy Dean, and first place was just a victory away. It was past 5:30 the next day, September 28—"very dark by then," in Hartnett's words—with the score 5-5 in the last of the ninth, two out, the bases empty. This surely would be the last inning before the game would be called. Hartnett stepped in against Pirates relief specialist Mace Brown. He swung and missed. He fouled off the next one. And then ... "When I got to second base," Hartnett recalled, "I couldn't see third for the players and fans there. I don't think I walked a step to the plate—I was carried in." The Cubs were on top. Three days later, they did win the pennant.

Merkle's baserunning blunder against the Cubs
1908

MOMENT

2 The story always focuses on the "bone-head" play of Giants rookie Fred Merkle in a crucial game against Chicago. But the alert Cubs deserve some credit. On September 23, 1908, after hitting a ninth-inning single that advanced a teammate to third base, Merkle ignored the formality of touching second base when Al Bridwell delivered an apparent game-winning hit. Second baseman Johnny Evers screamed for the ball. It wound up in the hands of the Giants' Joe McGinnity. Evers and teammate Joe Tinker wrestled him for it. McGinnity threw the ball into the crowd. Cubs Harry Steinfeldt and Rube Kroh braved the hostile Polo Grounds fans and grabbed it. The relay went to Tinker, then to Evers, who touched second. Manager Frank Chance pleaded with umpire Hank O'Day. The crowd surrounded them. Police helped them off the field. In the safety of his dressing room, O'Day rendered his decision: *Forceout.* Score still tied, 1-1. Game called because of near-riot. Two weeks later, when the 154-game regular season was scheduled to be at an end, the Cubs and Giants were deadlocked at 98-55. The "Merkle game" was replayed on October 8. Despite reported death threats and bribe attempts, despite a clamoring New York mob outside and an unruly crowd inside, the Cubs won, 4-2, as Mordecai "Three Finger" Brown relieved in the first inning and outpitched Christy Mathewson.

First baseman Fred Merkle, later a Cub, played 16 seasons in the majors.

The Bartman game

October 14, 2003

MOMENT

3

With a three-games-to-one lead in the 2003 National League Championship Series, the Cubs could have clinched a World Series spot by winning Game 5 or Game 7. With a 3-0 lead and five outs to go in Game 6, they could have won that one, too, even after a Marlins hitter stayed alive when Cubs left fielder Moises Alou couldn't make a difficult play, reaching into the stands on a foul fly ball. None of those things happened, and Cubs lore, for now and for a long time, puts the turning point at the hand of Steve Bartman, the 26-year-old, Cubs cap-wearing, headphone-listening fan who got in Alou's way with one on and one out in the eighth inning. Then came: walk, single, error, double … on and on the Marlins went until they had scored eight runs in the inning. Bartman had to leave the stands under protection. He was identified, then vilified by fans and politicians and comedians. He became a Halloween costume, the butt of Internet jokes and a metaphor for the Cubs' historic failings. The ball he deflected eventually sold for more than $100,000—and was ceremoniously blown up before the 2004 baseball season.

Leon Durham's misplay in the 1984 NLCS

Seventh inning in San Diego, October 7, 1984. Best-of-five National League

MOMENT

4

Championship Series even at two games apiece. Cubs leading, 3-2. Baseball's best pitcher that year on the mound as the Padres bat. Man on second, one out. Rick Sutcliffe induces obscure infielder Tim Flannery to hit a ground ball to the right side of the infield….

Now, first baseman Leon Durham was a good player. Earlier in this game, his two-run homer had staked the

Usually sure-handed, the Cubs' Leon Durham let a ground ball skip through his legs in the disastrous seventh inning of Game 5 against the Padres.

Cubs to a lead. Ninety-nine point four percent of the times he had a fielding chance in 1984, he performed his task without an error. This time, the ball skipped off the infield grass and through his legs. To Cubs fans, it seemed to roll forever. Carmelo Martinez, notoriously slow, had plenty of time to score the tying run. In a year in which everything had gone right for the Cubs, everything suddenly went wrong. A checked-swing single, a bad-hop double, another single. Sutcliffe was gone, and so were the Cubs' chances to go to the World Series. The Padres won, 6-3.

MOMENT

5 # Ruth's called shot, 1932 World Series

They were unfriendly World Series rivals. The Yankees were angry because the "cheapskate" Cubs had voted only a half share of Series loot to their ex-teammate, shortstop Mark Koenig, who had helped the Cubs to the 1932 pennant after they got him from the minor leagues in early August. And on this day at Wrigley Field, Game 3 on October 1, Chicago bench jockeys and fans were riding Babe Ruth, still a star at 37. Ruth responded with a three-run homer in the first inning. In the fifth, score tied, 4-4, Ruth came to bat against Charlie Root. Ruth grinned, took a strike, and gestured toward the Cubs. He took two balls, then watched another strike. He grinned, raised his hand again, shouted at Root. He hit the next pitch deep into the center field bleachers. The legend: He called his shot. The consensus: Ruth did taunt the Cubs, but did not point to the spot where he intended to hit the ball. Still, writers and Ruth himself recognized a good story, and the legend became one of baseball's most famous. Over the years, Ruth himself variously confirmed and denied it—and clearly enjoyed it.

Artist Robert Thom offered his take on one of baseball's great legends.

MOMENT

⑥

2003: Winning a postseason series after a 95-year drought

In October 1908, Ford assembled its first Model T in Detroit. The same month in the same city, Chicago beat the hometown baseball team in the World Series. Ninety-five years and more than a quarter-billion Fords later, the Cubs next won a series played after the end of the regular season. Little wonder the event—still two steps from a world championship—occasioned unprecedented glee for Cubs fans. Little wonder many of them flew to Atlanta for the deciding fifth game of the 2003 National League Division Series, wearing bright blue and overwhelming blasé Braves fans on the night of October 5 with "Let's Go, Cubs." "It was almost like we were playing a home game," said Cubs closer Joe Borowski, who finished the 5-1 victory for Kerry Wood. The Cubs players seemed as giddy as the rooters, several spraying their fans with champagne. By now, the fans were chanting "Dusty, Dusty." Revived under new manager Dusty Baker, armed with strong young pitchers and powerful veteran hitters, supplied with slick late-season additions, the Cubs were winners in October again.

INNING

The Sandberg game

June 23, 1984

Want to write base-ball fiction? Set it in the most beloved ballpark, packed

M O M E N T

7

to capacity, of course. Make the opponent your fiercest rival, the Cardinals. Have it the Saturday game of the week on national television. Put the good guys in a big hole—per-haps 7-1 in the second inning. And then create a hero. He should be young, handsome, clean-cut. We'll call him Ryne Sandberg. We'll have him get hit after hit as his team strug-gles back. He'll come to bat in the last of the ninth, his team behind by a run. He'll hit a homer off the best relief pitcher in the game, a former member of our team (call him

Ryne Sandberg's heroics against St. Louis seemed almost like make-believe.

Bruce Sutter). We need more drama: Have the Cardinals score two in the 10th. Our man comes up again against Sutter, one man on. He'll hit another homer. Tie game again. That gives him five hits, seven runs batted in. Finally, for our ending: A most forgettable player (we'll give him the name Dave Owen) comes through with the game-winning hit in the 11th inning. Cubs win, 12-11.

⑧ Turning on the lights

August 8, 1988

"I felt the game should be played in daylight," owner P.K. Wrigley said once. At other times, he explained the absence of lights at the ball field named by his father in terms of the surrounding neighborhood: "How can anybody sleep … ?" But 40 years after Wrigley Field stood as the last unlit major league park, ownership had changed, as had baseball economics. The commissioner had threatened to move future Cubs postseason games (television contracts, you know). There was politicking with the city, opposition from neighborhood groups, indignation from traditionalists ("… like putting aluminum siding on the Sistine Chapel"). On easy-to-remember 8/8/88, the Cubs drew a full house, including 532 media representatives, for a game between also-ran teams. A 91-year-old fan turned on the lights. Billy Williams and Ernie Banks threw out first balls. Morganna the Kissing Bandit bussed Ryne Sandberg. The game's first batter, the Phillies' Phil Bradley, homered off Rick Sutcliffe. After two innings, the wind blew. After 3½, the rain came. After a delay of 2 hours and 10 minutes, the game was postponed, with the Cubs leading, 3-1, and the gags about divine ire abundant. On 8/9/88, the Cubs defeated the Mets, 6-4. Under the lights.

Originally scheduled for 3:05 p.m., the Aug. 8 game was switched to night in an announcement made in June.

M O M E N T

The Cubs' fly-ball phobia
1929, 1969, 1998

There's a pattern here: In Philadelphia, in Game 4 of the 1929 World Series, the Cubs took an 8-0 lead into the seventh inning and appeared certain of tying the Series at two games each. Then, center fielder Hack Wilson lost two fly balls in the sun, left fielder Riggs Stephenson just missed catching another fly and the Athletics scored 10 runs in the inning. The A's won that October 12 game and wrapped up the Series in Game 5. In New York, on July 8, 1969, Ferguson Jenkins was pitching a one-hitter for the first-place Cubs and had a 3-1 lead entering the ninth inning. Center fielder Don Young misjudged one fly ball and dropped another. The Mets won the game and, eventually, the pennant and World Series. In Milwaukee, on September 23, 1998, as the Cubs strove for a post-season spot, they led 7-5 with two out in the Brewers' ninth. Left fielder Brant Brown dropped a fly ball with the bases loaded and the Cubs lost the game and their wild-card lead. They finished the season in a tie for the wild card and won a playoff but, drained, were swept by the Braves in the Division Series.

Brant Brown's muff in a key 1998 game in Milwaukee left Cubs fans in a state of shock.

st
rmances

PERFORMANCE

① **Cubs win 1907 and 1908 World Series titles**

Only the Yankees have won more World Series titles than the Cardinals. Yet St. Louis has never taken two in a row. The storied Dodgers haven't pulled off the back-to-back feat, either. In fact, only seven franchises can boast of doing that. The Cubs are one of them—and they were the first to do it. The 1907 team, which lost two straight games only once in the first 2½ months of the season, finished 107-45 and won the pennant by 17 games as Orval Overall, Three Finger Brown and Carl Lundgren combined for 61 victories and 21 shutouts. After the Cubs and Tigers played to a tie in the Series opener, Chicago swept to four straight wins— games in which Jack

Pfiester, Ed Reulbach, Overall and Brown allowed a total of three runs. Third baseman Harry Steinfeldt batted .471 against Detroit. The next year, the Cubs needed a bit of luck (Fred Merkle's blunder) to reach the Series, but once there they again dominated Ty Cobb and the Tigers. Brown (29 regular-season victories) and Overall each won twice and manager Frank Chance hit .421 as the Cubs prevailed, four games to one.

2

Hack Wilson hits 56 home runs, drives in 191 runs

Sure, as the game's historians point out, the ball took a pounding in 1930. But no one mashed it quite like the Cubs' Lewis "Hack" Wilson. No slouch the season before when he hit 39 home runs and knocked in a league-leading 159 runs, Wilson was off the charts in '30. Standing just 5-6, the outfielder slammed a National League-record 56 home runs, 16 more than the league runner-up that year, Chuck Klein. And he set a big-league record that still stands with 191 runs batted in, beating Klein by 21 for that season's N.L. RBI crown. Plus, Wilson batted .356. Through July, he had the already-staggering total of 104 RBIs. Then, he went on an unfathomable tear in August, driving in 53 runs in 30 games. For good measure, Wilson tacked on 34 RBIs in 26 games in September, far surpassing Lou Gehrig's 3-year-old major league record of 175 RBIs. In June, Wilson hit for the cycle against Philadelphia; in July, he had a three-homer game, also against the Phillies; in August, his 44th homer of the season, against Pittsburgh, broke the league record established in 1929 by the Phils' Klein. Listed at 190 for nearly seven decades, Wilson's runs-batted-in total was increased by one when research uncovered a missing RBI in a July game.

INNING

Ernie Banks captures back-to-back MVP awards

Until 1958, no recipient of a major league Most Valuable Player award had played on a team with a losing record. Until 1959, no National Leaguer had ever won consecutive MVP honors. Ernie Banks rewrote history with the flick of his wrists. Playing for sub-.500 clubs that tied for fifth place in both seasons, Banks led the league in home runs and RBIs in 1958 with totals of 47 and 129 and was second in homers (45) and tops again in RBIs (143) in 1959. He batted over .300 both seasons, led N.L. shortstops in fielding percentage in '59 and didn't miss a game either year. The result: two straight MVPs. While those were standout seasons, they were just part of his glittering body of work. A man whose talents and sunny personality combined to make him Mr. Cub, Banks hit 40 or more homers in four straight years (and five times overall), set a still-existing N.L. record for grand slams in one season (five, 1955) and won a Gold Glove. In the days before the proliferation of hitter-friendly ballparks, Banks became a member of a truly exclusive club in 1970 when he hit his 500th career homer. He was only the ninth man in major league history to reach that milestone.

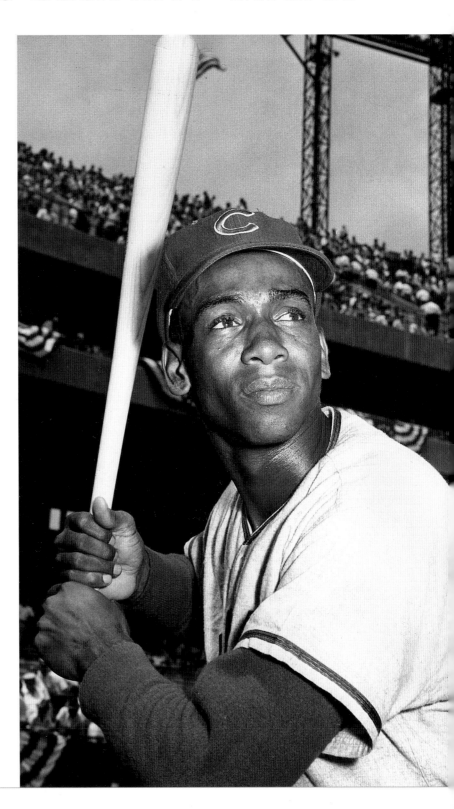

Sammy Sosa wallops 66 homers

Sammy Sosa did not win the Great Home Run Race of 1998. He did come out first in the hearts of many fans, though, because of his infectious grin and what-great-fun-this-is approach to his spirited battle with Mark McGwire. Yes, the Cardinals' McGwire got to 62 home runs first, thereby breaking Roger Maris' record, but Sosa eventually caught him at 62, again at 63 and once more at 65. And Sammy moved ahead, ever so briefly, when he cracked No. 66 at Houston on the night of September 25, only to lose out when McGwire homered moments later in St. Louis and then belted four over the last two games. On the way to his 66

home runs (and a league-leading 158 RBIs), Sosa set a big-league record with 20 home runs in one month (June) and went on an astounding May-June spree of 21 homers in a 22-game stretch. The '98 N.L. MVP, Sosa hit 63 homers the next season and connected for 64 in 2001. He is the only player in major league history with three 60-homer seasons.

The 1998 Great Home Run Race between Sammy Sosa and Mark McGwire was a feel-good story that captivated the baseball world.

1935 Cubs win 21 consecutive games in September, take pennant

PERFORMANCE

5 The Cubs were in third place entering play on September 4, 1935, 2½ games behind the first-place Cardinals and one-half game in back of the second-place Giants. Hoping to go on a nice spurt and overtake the league's top teams, Charlie Grimm's Cubs outdid themselves. Having started a long homestand with a victory and a loss, the Cubs then won 18 straight games at Wrigley Field. That shot them three games ahead of the defending World Series champion Cards with a five-game, season-ending series remaining at Sportsman's Park. (New York had fallen out of the race.) The Cubs made it 19 in a row when Lon Warneke tossed a two-hitter and 19-year-old Phil Cavarretta hit a second-inning homer off the Cards' Paul Dean, giving Chicago a 1-0 victory. Then, in the first game of a September 27 doubleheader, the Cubs pounded Dizzy Dean for 15 hits and clinched the pennant with their 20th consecutive triumph, 6-2 behind Bill Lee's six-hit pitching (his 20th win of the season) and Freddie Lindstrom's four hits and three RBIs. Chicago extending its winning streak to 21 games in the meaningless nightcap, then lost the final two games of the season. The World Series was a disappointment, though, Detroit a winner in six games.

Phil Cavarretta (right photo) homered to give Chicago its 19th straight victory and Bill Lee (middle, above, with Billy Jurges, left, and Billy Herman) pitched the pennant-clinching 20th win in a row.

Kerry Wood strikes out 20

Cubs righthander Kerry Wood, 20 years old and possessing extraordinary promise, possessed only a 2-2 major league record and 5.89 ERA when he took the mound for his fifth career start on May 6, 1998, against Houston at Wrigley Field. Wood got off to a terrific start that Wednesday afternoon, striking out the side in the first inning. But the young man had shown wildness after being summoned from Class AAA in April, walking 10 batters in his first $11\frac{1}{3}$ innings with the Cubs, so there were questions about how long he could keep his fastball harnessed. Not to worry.

PERFORMANCE

6

A hug by Mark Grace and a pat from catcher Sandy Martinez tell a nearly disbelieving Kerry Wood that, yes, he pitched a classic.

Wood struck out two hitters in the second inning and one in the third, an inning in which the Astros' Ricky Gutierrez grounded an infield hit off third baseman Kevin Orie's glove. The heat kept coming—the radar gun reached 100 miles per hour—and so did the strikeouts. Two Houston batters fanned in the fourth, three in the fifth. In the sixth, Wood allowed his second and last baserunner—he hit Craig Biggio with a pitch—but he also rang up strikeout No. 12. Then came a blazing finish, with Wood striking out the side in the seventh and eighth and getting two more Astros swinging in the ninth. Wood had set a National League record with 20 strikeouts, winning a 2-0 game in which he allowed one hit and did not walk a batter.

PERFORMANCE

1906 Cubs ring up 116 victories

Two weeks into the 1906 season, the Cubs had split 12 games. Not exactly the start envisioned by Frank Chance, who was in his first full season as manager. Chance was guiding an already-talented team bolstered by the offseason acquisitions of outfielder Jimmy Sheckard and third baseman Harry Steinfeldt. Also new to the club was lefthander Jack Pfiester, who had pitched briefly and unimpressively for the Pirates in 1903 and 1904 and was uncovered in the minors. Expectations began to be realized when the club reeled off a 10-game winning streak and slipped into first place. The team continued to play well, and it played better yet after obtaining pitchers Orval Overall from Cincinnati in June and Jack Taylor from St.

Louis in July. The club stood 68-30 on August 4. As gaudy as that mark was, folks hadn't seen anything yet. Chance's team won 37 of its next 39 games; by season's end, the Cubs were 116-36 and owned a victory total that stood alone as a major league record until Seattle equaled it 95 years later in a 162-game schedule. Three Finger Brown won 26 games, Pfiester 20, Ed Reulbach 19 and Carl Lundgren 17 for the runaway N.L. champions. Overall and Taylor (in his second tour with the Cubs) went a combined 24-6. Steinfeldt led the team in hitting (.327) and the league in RBIs (83). Reulbach tossed a one-hitter in the World Series and Brown a two-hitter, yet the underdog White Sox won in six games.

PERFORMANCE

In-season acquisitions Hank Borowy and Rick Sutcliffe spark title drives

The Cubs were in first place in the National League on July 27, 1945, when they bought righthanded pitcher Hank Borowy from the Yankees. And they were atop the N.L. East on June 13, 1984, when they obtained righthander Rick Sutcliffe from the Indians. Still, Borowy and Sutcliffe were seen as difference-makers, guys who could turn hopeful situations into done deals. They did just that. Borowy, somehow deemed expendable by the Yankees despite his 10-5 record for New York in '45 (and a 56-30 mark since reaching the majors in 1942), made 14 starts for Chicago and compiled an 11-2 record with a 2.13 earned-run average. His contribution was critical—the Cubs won the pennant by three games over St. Louis. Sutcliffe had won 17 games for Cleveland in 1983 but was 4-5 with a 5.15 ERA in '84 when the Indians unloaded him in a multiplayer deal in which they obtained promising outfielder Joe Carter. Sutcliffe dominated for the Cubs, going 16-1 and winning 14 consecutive games for a team that won the East Division by 6½ games over the Mets. Borowy pitched the Cubs' 1945 pennant-clinching game at Pittsburgh; Sutcliffe pitched the Cubs' 1984 division clincher—a two-hitter—in the same city.

Linked in Cubs history, Hank Borowy (above) and Rick Sutcliffe were remarkable difference-makers.

PERFORMANCE

Ed Reulbach hurls two shutouts in a doubleheader

Starting, completing and winning both games of a doubleheader was not unheard of in 1908. In fact, two American League pitchers turned the trick in the days just before and just after Ed Reulbach took the mound for the Cubs in both ends of a doubleheader at Brooklyn on September 26. One remarkable thing about Reulbach's heavy-duty workload was that it came in the heat of a pennant race—the "Merkle game" against the Giants had occurred just three days earlier. Even more remarkable: Reulbach pitched shutouts in both games, the only time the feat has been accomplished in major league history. In the opening game at Washington Park, Reulbach tossed a five-hitter as the Cubs won, 5-0. In the 1-hour, 12-minute second game, Big Ed was even more effective, yielding only three hits in a 3-0 victory. The double-shutout effort highlighted a stretch in which the righthander did not allow a run over 44 consecutive innings. Reulbach's late-season heroics helped the Cubs stay in the pennant fight with the Giants and Pirates, a battle that ended with Chicago defeating New York in a winner-take-all makeup game and the Cubs finishing one game ahead of both teams.

Mark Grace goes on an NLCS rampage

First baseman Mark Grace, a second-year major leaguer, had just helped Don Zimmer's surprising Cubs win the 1989 N.L. East title, showing the poise of a veteran while contributing a .314 batting average, 13 home runs and 79 RBIs. Still, Grace had never played amid the pressure of the postseason spotlight, so no one knew what to expect from him in the National League Championship Series against the Giants. From the start, Grace was calm, not jittery; confident, not apprehensive; great, not merely good. He collected 11 hits—including three doubles, a triple and a home run—in 17 at-bats and drove in eight runs. In the NLCS opener the first nighttime postseason game in Wrigley Field history, Grace hit a two-run homer in the first inning and collected three hits in four at-bats. He was 3-for-4 again in Game 2, driving in four runs. In Games 3, 4 and 5 in San Francisco, Grace went 2-for-3, 1-for-3 (with two RBIs) and 2-for-3. Alas, Grace's first base counterpart, Will Clark, put on his own show. Clark, playing with a stronger supporting cast, hit .650 to Grace's .647, had two homers (including a grand slam) among his 13 hits and also finished with eight RBIs. San Francisco won the series, four games to one.

In 129 seasons of Cubs baseball, there have been bright spots (such as the pennant won by Cap Anson's 1886 team) and disappointments (such as the third-place finish of the highly touted 2004 club, right).

CHAMPIONS OF THE UNITED STATES

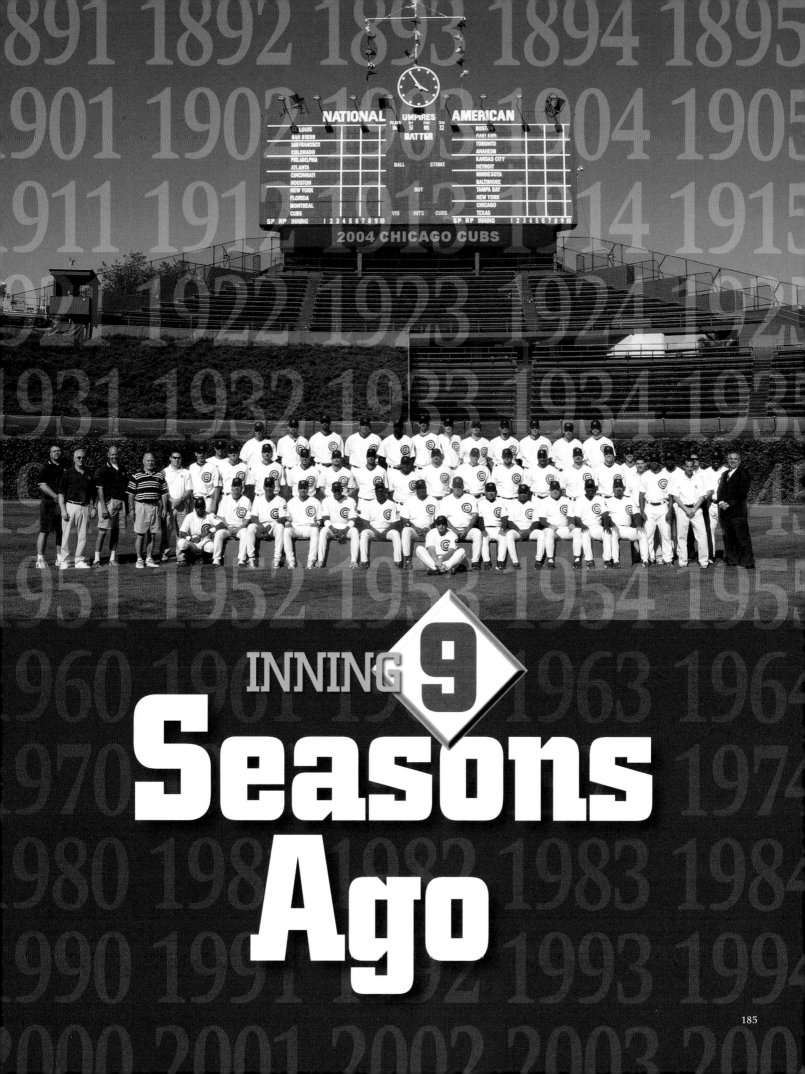

INNING 9

Seasons Ago

1876

Baseball's first recognized "major league," the eight-team National League, begins play on April 22. ... Chicago's N.L. franchise, called the White Stockings but later to be known as the Cubs, plays its first game on April 25 at Louisville and wins, 4-0, behind manager **Albert Spalding**, who pitches the first shutout in league history. ... Chicago wins the pennant with a 52-14 record. ... Spalding is 47-13 in a day of yeoman pitching performances. ... Chicago second baseman **Ross Barnes** hits the first-ever N.L. home run on May 2 against Cincinnati. It is his only homer of the season. ... Four Chicagoans finish in the top five in the league batting race, with Barnes hitting a league-high .404. ... First baseman **Cal McVey** has a 30-game hitting streak. ... The team plays its home games at the 23rd Street Grounds (23rd and State streets).

1877

Chicago slips to a 26-33 record and fifth-place in the N.L., which fields only six teams this season.

1878

New manager **Bob Ferguson** guides Chicago to a 30-30 record and a fourth-place finish. ... The club begins a seven-year stint at Lakefront Park (south of Randolph St. between Michigan Ave. and the Illinois Central Railroad tracks).

1879

Cap Anson, a regular in the Chicago lineup since the opening game in 1876, takes over as manager. He also plays first base and bats a league-leading .407. ... The club again winds up fourth, winning 46 games and losing 33.

1880

Chicago wins at a stunning pace, posting 67 victories in 84 games. The .798 winning percentage remains the best figure ever posted by a National League or American League team. ... From June 5 through July 8, the club wins 20 consecutive games. A victory and a tie precede the streak. ... Rookie righthander **Larry Corcoran** makes 60 starts, pitches 57 complete games and wins 43 of 57 decisions as Chicago wins the pennant by 15 games. ... Corcoran pitches a no-hitter against Boston on August 19. ... Outfielder **George Gore**'s .360 mark leads N.L. hitters.

1881

Anson's .399 batting average paces the N.L. ... Chicago again is the N.L. champion, this time with a 56-28 record.

1882

Chicago (55-29) wins its third consecutive pennant. ... Corcoran tosses his second career no-hitter, stopping Worcester on September 20. ... Anson's team and Cincinnati's American Association champions meet for postseason honors, but the series is called off after the clubs from the two wrangling leagues split the first two games.

1883

A 59-39 record relegates Chicago to second place as Boston ends the title run of Anson's team. ... In a May 22 game against Boston, Chicago outfielder **Billy Sunday** strikes out four times in his first major league game. ... The club sets a still-standing major league record for hits and runs in one inning, getting 18 of each in the seventh inning of a 26-6 pasting of Detroit on September 6.

1884

In the N.L.'s first schedule of more than 100 games, Chicago fashions a 62-50 mark and ties for fourth place. ... Third baseman **Ned Williamson** cracks 27 home runs, which stands as the major league record until **Babe Ruth** hits 29 for the Boston Red Sox in 1919. ... Williamson records the first three-homer game in major league history on May 30 and Anson matches the feat on August 6. ... Corcoran fires his third no-hitter, this one against Providence on June 27.

1885

Chicago returns to the top of the N.L., rolling to an 87-25 record. ... The club wins 18 straight games in June. ... Righthander **John Clarkson** posts 53 victories, pitches 623 innings and hurls a no-hitter. ... The team has a new home field: West Side Park (Congress and Throop streets). ... Anson's charges and St. Louis of the American Association play to a standoff in their postseason championship series, the teams splitting six games and tying the other contest.

1886

Chicago (90-34) wins its sixth pennant in the 11-year history of the N.L. but loses a postseason rematch with the American Association's St. Louis franchise. ... Anson's team wins 52 of 62 games at home. ... Outfielder/catcher **Mike "King" Kelly** (.388) is the league batting champion.

1887

In a season in which bases on balls count as hits, Anson posts an N.L.-best batting average of .421. ... Chicago's winning percentage drops from the 1886 figure of .726 to .587, the club going 71-50 and finishing third. ... Sunday plays his fifth and last season with Chicago,

John Clarkson

the feat on May 30 against Brooklyn. He wins by 6-4 and 11-7 scores. ... **Pat Luby** wins 17 consecutive decisions on the way to a 20-9 mark. ... Chicago, which winds up in second place, wins 19 of 20 games in an August/September stretch.

1891

The Chicago club divides its home season between West Side Park and South Side Park (35th and Wentworth streets). ... It's nearly a repeat performance in the standings. Chicago again finishes second, this time with an 82-53 record. ... Hutchison wins 43 games.

1892

South Side Park is now the exclusive home of the Chicago team. ... The National League expands to 12 teams, absorbing four franchises from the American Association, which ceases play after 10 seasons. ... The N.L. adopts a split-season

Bill Hutchison

appearing in 50 games. He later becomes a noted evangelist.

1888

Chicago inches up to second place with a 77-58 record. ... The walks-as-hits rule is abandoned after one season and Anson's batting average plummets 78 points. Still, the Chicago manager wins his fourth N.L. hitting crown. ... Outfielder **Hugh Duffy** breaks into the majors, hitting .282 for Chicago in 71 games. He wins

fame six years later by hitting a major league-record .438 for Boston's N.L. club.

Hugh Duffy

1889

Nursing a 64-65 mark in the final days of the season, Chicago averts a losing record in its last four games by winning three times and tying once.

1890

Righthander **Bill Hutchison**, 16-17 as a rookie in 1889, compiles a 42-25 record as the club improves to 83-53. ... Hutchison pitches two complete-game victories on one day, accomplishing format. Chicago finishes 31-39 (eighth place) in the first half, 39-37 (seventh) in the second half, becoming the first Anson team with a losing record. ... In the first six weeks of the season, the club experiences a nine-game losing streak and a 13-game winning streak. ... Anson's batting average dips to a career-low .275 as Chicago's offense proves a bust. ... Second baseman **Jimmy Canavan** hits .166 in 439 at-bats.

1893

The split-season concept is abandoned. ... Chicago struggles to a 56-71, ninth-place finish. ... West Side Grounds, at Polk and Lincoln (now Wolcott) streets, is used for Sunday-only games.

1894

Infielder **Bill Dahlen** reels off a 42-game batting streak. Through the 2004 season, it is the fourth-longest streak in major league history. ... Chicago's winning percentage (.432) is the worst in franchise history and the club is mired in seventh place at 57-75. ... West Side Grounds becomes the club's full-time home.

1895

Righthander **Clark Griffith** wins 25 games for a fourth-place Chicago team that goes 72-58. ... Third-year outfielder **Bill Lange** hits .389.

Tom Burns

1896

On July 13, Philadelphia's **Ed Delahanty** slams four homers off Chicago's **Adonis Terry**. Yet Terry comes out a 9-8 winner. ... Anson, at age 44, bats .335 for Chicago, which finishes fifth at 71-57.

1897

Anson winds up his Chicago career. In his 22nd season as a player and 19th year as manager, he hits .303 and directs the team to a 59-73 record (ninth place).

1898

Tom Burns, a Chicago infielder from 1880 through 1891, succeeds Anson as manager. He guides the club to an 85-65 record and a jump to fourth place. ... Griffith is 26-10. ... **Frank Chance** breaks into the majors on April 29 as a late-game catching replacement for Chicago's **Tim Donahue**. ...On August 21, Walter Thornton no-hits Brooklyn.

1899

A strong start helps lure the city's largest baseball

crowd to date—27,489. The fans see Chicago beat St. Louis, 4-0, on April 30. ... The team fades to eighth place, winning 75, losing 73.

1900

Tom Loftus, whose major league managerial resume featured stints in the Union Association, American Association and National League (and eventually would include the American League), becomes Chicago's manager. ... The N.L. cuts back to eight teams. ... Loftus' club (65-75) ties St. Louis for fifth place.

1901

Chicago endures its worst N.L. season to date, going 53-86 (.381). The club finishes sixth.

1902

The Chicago franchise, called the White Stockings, Orphans, Colts and a number of other names over the years, also is referred to as the Cubs. ... **Frank Selee**, who in the previous 12 years had managed Boston to five N.L. pennants, takes the reins of the Cubs. His first Chicago team goes 68-69 and ends up fifth. ... Shortstop **Joe Tinker** makes his big-league debut in the April 17 season opener at Cincinnati. He collects a double in four at-bats and handles four fielding chances flawlessly. ... **Johnny Evers** breaks into the majors on September 1, playing shortstop in a double-header at Philadelphia. Tinker is stationed at third base and **Bobby Lowe** mans second base. Evers has a shaky debut, going 1-for-7 and making three errors. ... The first Tinker-to-Evers-to-Chance double play is recorded in the second game of a September 14 doubleheader against Cincinnati.

1903

Chance, heretofore used more as a catcher and outfielder than as a first baseman, settles in at first for the Cubs and Evers is a regular at second. Tinker plays primarily at shortstop, as he did in '02, with occasional duty at third base. ... Chance hits .327 and shares the league lead in stolen bases with 67. ... The Cubs improve to 82-56 and claim third place. ... In a December trade with N.L. rival St. Louis, Chicago acquires pitcher **Mordecai "Three Finger" Brown**, who is coming off a rookie season in which he compiled a 9-13 record.

1904

The Cubs post an impressive 93-60 record but wind up 13 games behind the pennant-winning Giants. ... On June 11, **Bob Wicker** hurls a no-hitter over 9⅓ innings against the Giants. **Sam Mertes** breaks up the gem with a single, but Wicker winds up with a one-hit, 1-0 victory in 12 innings. ... Outfielders **Frank "Wildfire" Schulte** and

Solly Hofman first appear in Cubs uniforms.

1905

With Chicago in fourth place with a 52-38 record, Chance replaces Selee as manager. The Cubs go 40-23 the rest of the way and finish third. ... Brown, **Jake Weimer** and rookie **Ed Reulbach** all win 18 games.

1906

The Cubs win 116 games and finish 20 games ahead of the Giants in the N.L. pennant race. The victory total stands alone in the major league record book until Seattle equals the mark 95 years later. ... From August 6 through September 16, the Cubs run off winning streaks of 11, 14 and 12 games. The 37-2 run helps the Cubs increase their lead over second-place New York from 4½ games to 17½. ... Brown tosses 10 shutouts and wins 26 games. ... Heavily favored in the World Series, the Cubs are upset in six games by the White Sox.

1907

Chance's Cubs win the N.L. pennant by 17 games, then claim their first World Series title by defeating the Tigers, four games to none (with one tie). ... **Orval Overall**, obtained from Cincinnati in June 1906, goes 23-8. He tosses eight shutouts.... Brown is 20-6 for the 107-45 team. ...

Cubs opponents average only 2.4 runs.

1908

The Cubs repeat as World Series champions, downing Detroit in five games. ... Chicago (99-55) wins the pennant by defeating the Giants in a makeup of a September 23 game in which **Fred Merkle**'s mental lapse had turned an apparent New York victory over Chicago into a 1-1 tie. In the October 8 game to decide the title, Brown relieves **Jack Pfiester** in

Orval
Overall

the first inning and out-pitches **Christy Mathewson** in a 4-2 Cubs win. ... On September 26, Reulbach pitches shutouts in both games of a doubleheader at Brooklyn. He allows five hits in the opener and wins, 5-0, then permits only three hits while winning the nightcap, 3-0. ... Brown fashions a 29-9 record; Reulbach finishes 24-7.

1909

After winning 322 regular-season games and three pennants in the previous three seasons, the Cubs finish second despite winning 104 games. Pittsburgh rules the league by 6½ games with a 110-42 mark. ... **Johnny Kling**, the Cubs' No. 1 catcher since 1901, sits out the season in a contract dispute. ... Righthander **Leonard "King" Cole** makes his major league debut on the final day of the season and throws a six-hit shutout at St. Louis.

1910

Kling is back—and so are the Cubs. Chicago again wins 104 games, and this time it's good enough for a 13-game edge over second-place New York. ... On June 28, Tinker steals home twice in an 11-1 rout of Cincinnati. ... Schulte shares the league home run lead with 10. ... Brown notches 25 victories and Cole wins 20 of 24 decisions.

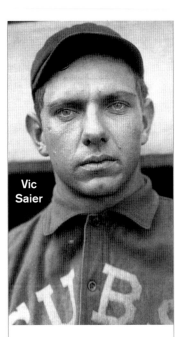

1911

Cubs second baseman **Heinie Zimmerman** hits two homers and drives in nine runs in a 20-2 pasting of Boston on June 11. ... Brown pitches in a career-high 53 games, goes 21-11. ... Schulte sets a major league record by hitting four grand slams. He leads the N.L. with 21 homers. ... The second-place Cubs are 92-62.

1912

Zimmerman, now playing third base, wins the Triple Crown. He leads the N.L. with a .372 batting average, 14 home runs and 103 RBIs (although RBIs don't become an official statistic until 1920). ... Rookie righthander **Larry Cheney** compiles a 26-10 record. ... Chicago is third in the N.L. standings at 91-59. ... In December, Tinker is traded to Cincinnati. He becomes the Reds' manager.

1913

Evers, coming off his best offensive season in the majors (.341 average), replaces Chance as manager. ... Righthander **Bert Humphries**, acquired in the Tinker deal, leads the N.L. in winning percentage (.800) with a 16-4 record. ... Cheney pitches a 14-hit shutout against the Giants on September 14. ... After Chicago's 88-65, third-place season, Evers is released and joins the Braves.

Vic Saier

1914

Hank O'Day is the Cubs' new manager. ... The club wins its final two games of the season to finish above .500. Chicago's 78-76 record is good for fourth place. ... First baseman **Vic Saier** challenges for the N.L. homer title, finishes second to Philadelphia's **Gavvy Cravath** with 18.

1915

The Cubs turn to **Roger Bresnahan** as their manager. ... Chicago's **Zip Zabel** pitches a major league-record 18⅓ innings in relief on June 17 as the Cubs defeat Brooklyn, 4-3, in 19 innings. ... **Jimmy Lavender** pitches a no-hitter against New York on August 31. ... The club dips below .500 for the first time since 1902, falling to 73-80. It manages a first-division finish, though, winding up a half-game ahead of the fifth-place Pirates. ... **James "Hippo" Vaughn** wins 20 games.

1916

Charles Weeghman, who had owned the Chicago Whales of the Federal League (which folded after the 1915 season), heads a syndicate that acquires the Cubs franchise from **Charles Taft**. **William Wrigley Jr.** invests $50,000 in the club. ... After 22 full seasons at West Side Grounds, the Cubs move into Weeghman Park (present-day Wrigley Field). The park had opened in 1914 as home of the Whales. ... The first N.L. game at Clark and Addison streets was played on April 20, with the Cubs edging Cincinnati, 7-6, in 11 innings. ... Tinker is back with the Cubs—as manager. He had managed the Whales the previous two years. ... **Three Finger Brown**, back with the Cubs after three seasons with other teams, and longtime pitching rival **Christy Mathewson** close out their playing careers by going head to head in a September 4 game in Chicago. Mathewson, a Giants star since the turn of the century and now manager of the Reds, is the winner in a 10-8 Cincinnati victory. ... The new home park proves to be not-so-friendly confines. The Cubs go 37-41 there on the way to a 67-86 mark that drops them to fifth place (19½ games behind the fourth-place Giants).

1917

Fred Mitchell becomes the Cubs' sixth manager in six seasons. ... Vaughn and Cincinnati's **Jim Toney** hook up in an unprecedented no-hit duel on May 2 in Chicago. Neither pitcher allows a hit through nine innings, but the Reds break through with two singles and an unearned run in the 10th and win, 1-0. ... A leg fracture sidelines first baseman Saier in April. To fill the void, the club obtains Merkle from Brooklyn. ... The Cubs again finish fifth but improve their record to 74-80.

1918

Vaughn (22 wins, eight shutouts), trade acquisition **Lefty Tyler** (19 victories, eight shutouts) and **Claude Hendrix** (19-7 record) power a formidable pitching staff. ... **Grover Alexander**, obtained in an offseason trade with the Phillies, misses most of the season because of military duty. ... Tyler pitches all 21 innings of a July 17 game against the Phillies and wins, 2-1. ... Rookie shortstop **Charlie Hollocher** leads the offense with a .316 batting average. Merkle hits .297. ... In a season shortened because of World War I, the Cubs post an 84-45 record and win the pennant by 10½

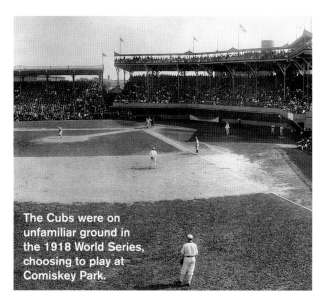

The Cubs were on unfamiliar ground in the 1918 World Series, choosing to play at Comiskey Park.

games. ... Pitchers **Carl Mays** and **Babe Ruth** each win two games as the Red Sox win the World Series over Chicago in six games. To enable more fans to attend, the Cubs play their home Series games at the White Sox's Comiskey Park, whose seating capacity of 30,000 is nearly twice that of Weeghman Park.

1919

Wrigley buys controlling interest of the team. ... The 75-65 Cubs finish third, 21 games behind the N.L. champion Reds. ... Vaughn wins 21 games, Alexander 16.

1920

Alexander fashions a 27-14 record but the Cubs struggle overall (75-79, tie for fifth). ... Weeghman Park is renamed Cubs Park.

1921

Wrigley is now sole owner of the Cubs, and Evers is back with the team as manager. ... After getting ready for the season at numerous locales over the years, the Cubs conduct spring training on Catalina Island, off the coast of southern California. They will train at Catalina for most of the next three decades. ... With the club buried in the second division, **Bill Killefer** replaces Evers in early August. ... Chicago's .418 winning percentage (64-89 record) is the second-worst in franchise history. ... Rookie first baseman **Ray Grimes** bats .321 for the seventh-place Cubs.

1922

Between games of a May 30 morning/afternoon doubleheader in Chicago, the Cubs deal outfielder **Max Flack** to the Cardinals for outfielder **Cliff Heathcote**. Flack goes 0-for-4 for the Cubs in the first game and 1-for-4 for the Cards in the nightcap; Heathcote is 0-for-3 for St. Louis, then 2-for-4 for the Cubs. ... On August 25 at Cubs Park, the Cubs outscore the Phillies, 26-23, in a game that establishes a still-standing record for most total runs scored in a major league game. In amassing their 49 runs, the two clubs combine for 51 hits. **Hack Miller** hits two home runs for the Cubs, who score 10 runs in the second inning and 14 in the fourth. ... Grimes hits .354 and Miller, who entered the season with only 15 games of major league experience, bats .352 in 466 at-bats. ... Hollocher finishes at .340 for the fifth-place Cubs (80-74).

1923

Chicago, 83-71, winds up fourth. ... Alexander wins 22 games. ... Hollocher is limited to 66 games because of health problems, but he bats .342.

The next day of the '22 season, the Cubs were shut out, 3-0, in 11 innings by the Phils.

1924

Alexander earns his 300th career victory, going the distance in a 12-inning, 7-3 Cubs triumph over the Giants on September 20 at the Polo Grounds. ... It's a fifth-place season (81-72) for Chicago. ... In October, the Cubs acquire shortstop **Rabbit Maranville** and first baseman **Charlie Grimm** from the Pirates.

The Cubs pulled a Rabbit out of the hat in a trade with Pittsburgh.

1925

On April 14, WGN's **Quin Ryan** describes the action of the Cubs-Pirates season opener from the grandstand roof at Cubs Park. Alexander not only wins that game, 8-2, he also contributes a single, double and home run. ... For the first time, the Cubs skid to last place, finishing 68-86 in a season during which Killefer, Maranville and **George Gibson** all serve as manager. ... Young catcher **Gabby**

Jimmy
Cooney

Hartnett slams 24 home runs. ... In October, the Cubs draft outfielder **Hack Wilson** off the Toledo roster. Wilson had seen major league duty with the Giants in 1923, 1924 and 1925, hitting 16 home runs in 172 games.

1926

Joe McCarthy, who had managed Louisville of the American Association the previous seven seasons, is manager of the Cubs. ... Wilson hits an N.L.-leading 21 homers. ... McCarthy guides the club back into the first division (fourth place, at 82-72). ... In December, club officials announce that Cubs Park is being renamed Wrigley Field.

1927

Wilson and the Phillies' **Cy Williams** finish with 30 home runs, tie for the N.L. title. ... The Cubs are the first N.L. franchise to attract one million fans. The attendance is 1,159,168. ... Left fielder **Riggs Stephenson** hits a league-leading 46 doubles and boasts a .344 average. ... On May 30 at Pittsburgh's Forbes Field, Cubs shortstop **Jimmy Cooney** makes an unassisted triple play. He snares **Paul Waner**'s liner, steps on second base to double up **Lloyd Waner** and tags out **Clyde Barnhart**, who was caught off first base. ... Eight days after his fielding gem, Cooney is traded to the Phillies. ... Righthander **Charlie Root**, in his second season with the Cubs, tops the N.L. in victories with 26. ... Chicago (85-68) again is fourth in the standings. ... Outfielder **Kiki Cuyler** is obtained from Pittsburgh in a post-season trade.

1928

Wilson clubs 31 homers, shares the N.L. lead with the Cardinals' **Jim Bottomley**. ... Cubs rookie righthander **Pat Malone** wins 18 games. ... The Cubs win 13 straight games in May. ... McCarthy's team challenges for the pennant, winds up third at 91-63. ... On November 7, the Cubs acquire seven-time N.L. batting titlist and reigning champion **Rogers Hornsby** from the Braves for five players and cash.

1929

Wilson knocks in an N.L.-high 159 runs and second baseman Hornsby drives in 149. Both slam 39 homers for a Cubs offense that also gets 110 RBIs from Stephenson, 102 from Cuyler and 91 from Grimm. ... Hornsby hits .380, Stephenson .362, Cuyler .360 and Wilson .345. ... Malone wins 22 games, Root 19 and **Guy Bush** 18. ... It all adds up to a 98-54 record and the Cubs' first pennant in 11 years. ... In the World Series, the Cubs blow an eight-run lead in the seventh inning

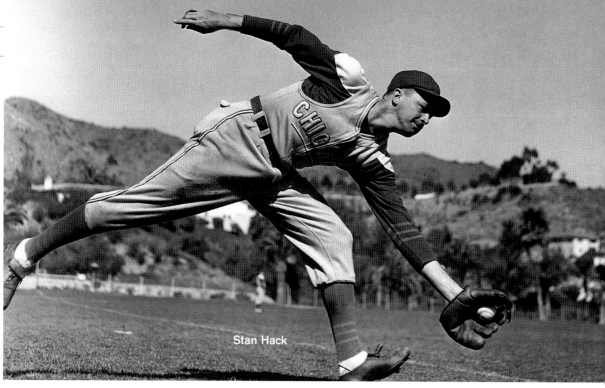
Stan Hack

of Game 4 and go on to lose in five games to the Philadelphia Athletics.

1930

Wilson sets an N.L. record with 56 home runs and establishes a major league mark with 190 runs batted in. He also hits .356. ... Sixty-nine years later, Wilson's RBI total is officially amended to 191 when research that uncovered a missing RBI is accepted. ... Wilson hits for the cycle against the Phillies on June 23. ... Cuyler has 134 RBIs and Hartnett 122. ... Malone shares the N.L. lead in wins with 20. ... The Cubs (90-64) finish two games behind the pennant-winning Cardinals.

1931

With McCarthy cut loose (he takes over as Yankees manager), Hornsby is the Cubs' field leader. ... Hornsby leads by example, smashing three homers and a single and driving in eight runs in

Chicago's 10-6 victory at Pittsburgh on April 24. ... Wilson's numbers take a plunge. He bats .261 and has 13 homers and 61 RBIs in 112 games. ... Promising second baseman **Billy Herman** joins the Cubs from the minor leagues and makes his big-league debut on August 29. ... Hornsby guides the club to an 84-70 record and third place. ... In November, Wilson is traded to the Cardinals.

1932

Owner Wrigley dies. His son, **Philip K. Wrigley**, succeeds him. ... With the season inching toward the 100-game mark and the Cubs in second place, management appoints Grimm to succeed Hornsby as manager. ... The club goes on to win the pennant, with a 14-game winning streak paving the way. Victory No. 12 in the string is remarkable. Trailing the Giants, 5-4, on August 31 at Wrigley Field, the Cubs tie

it in the ninth on Cuyler's two-out single. Then, after New York erupts for four runs in the 10th, the Cubs strike for five in their half of the inning, the final three coming on a Cuyler home run. The blast is Kiki's fifth hit of the day. ... Righthander **Lon Warneke** joins the Cubs' rotation at age 23 and leads the league in wins (22) and earned-run average (2.37). ... Bush posts 19 victories for the 90-64 Cubs. ... **Stan Hack** makes his Cubs debut. The third baseman, 22, appears in 72 games. ... Shortstop **Billy Jurges** is shot in an off-field incident in July but is back in the lineup in a little more than two weeks. ... Former Yankees shortstop **Mark Koenig**, obtained from the minors in August, hits .353 in 33 games. ... The team wears uniform numbers for the first time. ... The Cubs are vanquished in the World Series by the Yankees, whose four-game sweep features **Babe Ruth**'s alleged "called shot" home run.

1933

The Cubs get off to an 11-17 start, never quite recover and finish third. ... Bush wins 20 games and Warneke goes 18-13 with a 2.00 ERA. ... In his first season with the Cubs, outfielder **Babe Herman** drives in 93 runs. He has a big day on July 20 against the Phillies, walloping three home runs and a single and knocking in eight runs in a 10-1 Cubs romp. ... Chicago (86-68) finishes six games behind the pennant-winning Giants.

Babe Herman

1934

Chuck Klein, a Triple Crown winner in the N.L. in 1933, joins the club after a trade with the Phillies. He goes on to hit 20 homers and knock in 80 runs. ... The Cubs sign local high school star **Phil Cavarretta**, who attended nearby Lane Tech. After minor league stops at Peoria and Reading, first baseman Cavarretta makes his Cubs debut at age 18 on September 16. On September 25, his first

major league homer gives Bush a 1-0 victory over Cincinnati. ... Warneke finishes with 22 wins for a Chicago team that goes 86-65 (third place). ... Rookie **Bill Lee** wins 13 games and throws four shutouts.

1935

The Cubs win 100 games and upend the Gas House Gang Cardinals, the defending World Series champions, in the N.L. pennant race. ... Grimm's team wins 21

consecutive games in September. The 20th in that run, a 6-2 victory over St. Louis, clinches the flag. ... Hartnett hits .344 and **Billy Herman** has a .341 average. ... Klein drills 21 homers. ... Warneke and Lee are both

Billy Herman

20-game winners. ... Chicago is a World Series loser for the fifth time in its last five tries, falling to the Tigers in six games.

1936

Billy Herman gets three doubles and a home run and goes 5-for-5 on opening day as the Cubs win, 12-7, at St. Louis. ... Chicago reels off its second long winning streak in two seasons, 15 victories in a row in June. ... Lee and lefthander **Larry French** are 18-game winners, right fielder **Frank Demaree** bats .350 with 96 RBIs and Herman hits at a .334 clip. Still, the Cubs yield their N.L. championship to the Giants, finishing 87-67 and in a tie for second place. ... After the season, Chicago deals Warneke to the Cardinals in a trade that sends first baseman **Rip Collins** to the Cubs.

1937

On June 25, against the Dodgers, Cubs left fielder **Augie Galan** becomes the first player in N.L. history to hit home runs from both sides of the plate in the same game. ... Demaree collects six hits in seven at-bats in the first game of a July 5 doubleheader against the Cardinals. Three of Demaree's hits are doubles as the Cubs win, 13-12, in 14 innings at Wrigley Field. ... Hartnett's batting average is a career-high .354. ... Chicago is runner-up in the N.L. with a 93-61

record. ... In September, front-office man **Bill Veeck** plants ivy on the walls at Wrigley Field.

1938

Just before the start of the season, the Cubs acquire **Dizzy Dean** from the Cardinals. ... With the Cubs 5½ games out of first place, catcher Hartnett succeeds Grimm as manager on July 20. ... On September 28, with darkness descending on

In 1938, Dizzy Dean was 7-1 with a 1.81 ERA as a Cub. He threw one shutout—on April 24, against St. Louis.

Wrigley Field, Hartnett's ninth-inning "Homer in the Gloamin'" off Pittsburgh's **Mace Brown** enables the Cubs to wrest first place from the Pirates. Chicago holds the lead over the final four days of the season. ... Hack bats .320. ... Lee posts an N.L.-best 22 victories. ... **Clay Bryant** wins 19 games. ... At 89-63, the Cubs finish two games ahead of the Pirates. ... In a repeat of the only other Cubs-Yankees World Series, the Cubs lose four straight. Dean, 7-1 in the regular season, pitches creditably as Chicago's starter in Game 2 but yields a game-deciding home run to **Frank Crosetti** in the eighth inning. ... **Grover Alexander** is elected to the Baseball Hall of Fame.

1939

The Cubs' record (84-70) is only six games off the club's pennant-winning pace of 1938, yet Chicago drops to fourth in the standings. ... Outfielder **Hank Lieber**, acquired from the Giants,

ADRIAN CONSTANTINE ANSON
"CAP"
GREATEST HITTER AND GREATEST
NATIONAL LEAGUE PLAYER-MANAGER
OF 19TH CENTURY. STARTED WITH
CHICAGOS IN NATIONAL LEAGUE'S
FIRST YEAR 1876. CHICAGO MANAGER
FROM 1879 TO 1897, WINNING 5 PENNANTS.
WAS .300 CLASS HITTER 20 YEARS,
BATTING CHAMPION 4 TIMES.

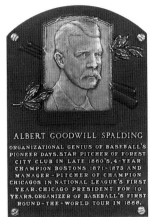

ALBERT GOODWILL SPALDING
ORGANIZATIONAL GENIUS OF BASEBALL'S
PIONEER DAYS. STAR PITCHER OF FOREST
CITY CLUB IN LATE 1860'S, 4-YEAR
CHAMPION BOSTONS 1871-1875 AND
MANAGER-PITCHER OF CHAMPION
CHICAGOS IN NATIONAL LEAGUE'S FIRST
YEAR. CHICAGO PRESIDENT FOR 10
YEARS. ORGANIZER OF BASEBALL'S FIRST
ROUND-THE-WORLD TOUR IN 1888.

hits 24 home runs. ... Lee is a 19-game winner. ... **Cap Anson** and **Albert Spalding** are elected to the Baseball Hall of Fame.

1940

Hartnett's team slips to fifth with a 75-79 record. ... Outfielder **Bill "Swish" Nicholson**, in his first full season as a Cubs regular, slams 25 home runs and knocks in 98 runs. ... Righthander **Claude Passeau**, obtained from the Phillies during the 1939 season, wins 20 games.

1941

Jimmie Wilson succeeds Hartnett as manager. ... On May 6, the Cubs trade Billy Herman to the Dodgers. ... Nicholson's power numbers (26 homers, 98 RBIs) mirror his 1940 performance. ... Hack hits .317 for the second consecutive year. ... The Cubs (70-84) drop to sixth in the standings. ... The club buys the steelwork and electrical cables necessary to install lights at Wrigley Field. But when the U.S. is drawn into

World War II, the Cubs donate the equipment to the military. Installation of lights remains on hold.

1942

Catcher **Paul Gillespie**, just up from Tulsa of the Texas League, becomes the first Cub to hit a home run in his first major league at-bat, connecting off the Giants' **Harry Feldman** in the second inning of a September 11 game. ... It's another down season (68-86), one in which the Cubs again finish sixth. ... Passeau's 19 wins are a bright spot.

1943

Andy Pafko makes his big-league debut on September 24 on a miserable, rainy day at Wrigley Field. Only 314 fans brave the elements. Pafko, who had hit .356 at Los Angeles of the Pacific Coast League, rewards the gathering with a single, double and four RBIs as the Cubs defeat the Phillies, 7-4, in a game halted in the fifth inning. ...

Bill Nicholson

Paul Gillespie

Nicholson tops the N.L. in home runs (29) and RBIs (128). ... Second-year man **Hi Bithorn** wins 18 games. ... The Cubs rise to fifth at 74-79.

1944

Nicholson again leads the league in homers (33) and runs batted in (122). ... Nicholson homers on his last at-bat in a July 22 game against the Giants at the Polo Grounds and hits three in a row in the first game of a July 23 doubleheader against New York, establishing an N.L. record with four consecutive home runs. In the

nightcap of the double-header, he homers in the seventh inning and then is walked intentionally with the bases loaded in the eighth. ... Grimm, who had been managing Milwaukee of the American Association since 1941, returns as Cubs manager after the club gets off to a 1-10 start. ... A 13-game losing streak marks the Cubs' 2-16 beginning to the season. ... Grimm gets the club going. The highlight: an 11-game winning streak that begins in late July. ... Third-year man **Hank Wyse** wins 16 games for a Chicago team that compiles a 75-79 record (fourth place).

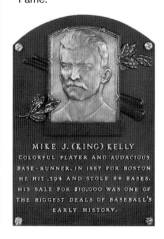

Don Johnson

1945

In fourth place at the end of June, Chicago goes on an 11-game winning streak beginning July 1 and moves into first place. ... Although boasting a four-game lead in the N.L. race more than halfway through the season, the Cubs opt to strengthen their pitching staff and purchase righthander **Hank Borowy** from the Yankees on July 27. Borowy, 10-5 for the Yankees, goes 11-2 with a 2.13 ERA for the Cubs and completes 11 of his 14 starts. ... The Cubs set a modern club record for hits in a game, collecting

28 in a 24-2 thrashing of Boston at Braves Field on July 3. Cavarretta and second baseman **Don Johnson** both go 5-for-7. The Cubs manage only one home run, by catcher **Mickey Livingston**. ... Ahead of second-place St. Louis by 1½ games with five games to play, the Cubs finish 5-0 and win the pennant by three games with a 98-56 record. ... Wyse wins 22 games and posts a 2.68 ERA. ... Passeau goes 17-9 with a 2.46 ERA. ... Cavarretta is the Cubs' first batting champion in 33 years. He hits .355. ... Hack contributes a .323 mark. ... Center fielder Pafko drives in 110 runs. ... Borowy's 9-0 triumph in Game 1 and Passeau's one-hitter in Game 3 are World Series highlights for the Cubs, who lose in seven games to the Tigers. ... **Mike "King" Kelly** is elected to the Baseball Hall of Fame.

MIKE J. (KING) KELLY
COLORFUL PLAYER AND AUDACIOUS
BASE-RUNNER. IN 1887 FOR BOSTON
HE HIT .394 AND STOLE 84 BASES.
HIS SALE FOR $10,000 WAS ONE OF
THE BIGGEST DEALS OF BASEBALL'S
EARLY HISTORY.

FRANK LEROY CHANCE
FAMOUS LEADER OF CHICAGO CUBS. WON PENNANT WITH CUBS IN FIRST FULL SEASON AS MANAGER IN 1906-THAT TEAM COMPILED 116 VICTORIES UNEQUALLED IN MAJOR LEAGUE HISTORY-ALSO WON PENNANTS WINNER IN 07 AND 08. STARTED WITH CHICAGO IN 1898. ALSO MANAGER NEW YORK A.L. AND BOSTON A.L.

JOHN JOSEPH EVERS
"THE TROJAN"
MIDDLE-MAN OF THE FAMOUS DOUBLE PLAY COMBINATION OF TINKER TO EVERS TO CHANCE. WITH THE PENNANT WINNING CHICAGO CUBS OF 1906-07-08-10 AND WITH THE BOSTON BRAVES' MIRACLE TEAM OF 1914. VOTED MOST VALUABLE PLAYER IN N.L. IN 1914. SERVED AS PLAYER, COACH AND MANAGER IN BIG LEAGUES AND AS A SCOUT FROM 1902 THROUGH 1934. SHARES RECORD FOR MAKING MOST SINGLES IN FOUR GAME WORLD SERIES.

JOSEPH B. TINKER
FAMOUS AS A MEMBER OF ONE OF BASEBALL'S GREATEST DOUBLE PLAY COMBINATIONS-FROM TINKER TO EVERS TO CHANCE. A BIG LEAGUER FROM 1902 THROUGH 1916 WITH THE CHICAGO CUBS AND CINCINNATI REDS AND THE CHICAGO FEDS. MANAGER CINCINNATI 1913 AND CHICAGO N.L. 1916. SHORTSTOP ON CUBS' TEAM THAT WON PENNANTS IN 1906,'07 '08 AND 1910.

MORDECAI PETER BROWN
(THREE-FINGERED AND MINER)
MEMBER OF CHICAGO N.L. CHAMPIONSHIP TEAM OF 1906,'07,'08,'10. A RIGHT HANDED PITCHER. WON 239 GAMES DURING MAJOR LEAGUE CAREER THAT ALSO INCLUDED ST. LOUIS AND CINCINNATI N.L. AND CUBS IN F.L. FIRST MAJOR LEAGUER TO PITCH FOUR CONSECUTIVE SHUTOUTS, ACHIEVING THIS FEAT ON JUNE 13, JUNE 25, JULY 2 AND JULY 4 IN 1908.

1946

While the Cardinals and Dodgers engage in a spirited pennant race that requires a playoff, the Cubs slip to third with an 82-71 record. ... No Cub hits more than eight home runs and only first baseman **Eddie Waitkus** is a .300 hitter (.304). ... Cavarretta, seeing extensive outfield duty, contributes a team-high 78 RBIs. ... **Frank Chance**, **Johnny Evers** and **Joe Tinker** are elected to the Baseball Hall of Fame.

1947

On May 18, **Jackie Robinson**'s first game at Wrigley Field as a member of the Dodgers draws a Cubs single-game paid attendance record of 46,572 fans. The mark still stands. ... Nicholson's 26-homer output is the highlight of a 69-85, sixth-place season. ... The American League edges the National, 2-1, in the first All-Star Game played at Wrigley Field. Two Cubs—Pafko and Cavarretta—appear in the game.

1948

Norman Rockwell's noted painting of a forlorn Cubs dugout appears on the cover of the September 4 *Saturday Evening Post*. ... Five days after the Post issue date, the Cubs begin a 10-game losing streak. ... Strong seasons by Pafko (26 homers, 101 RBIs) and lefthander **Johnny Schmitz** (18 victories) can't stave off a tumble into last place by the Cubs, whose record is 64-90. ... Lefthander **Bob "Dutch" McCall** loses 13 consecutive decisions.

1949

The Cubs' woes continue, and **Frankie Frisch** replaces Grimm as manager on June 12. ... At the trading deadline three days later, the Cubs send outfielders **Harry Walker** and **Peanuts Lowrey** to the Reds for outfielders **Hank Sauer** and **Frankie Baumholtz**. ... As a Cub, Sauer hits 27 homers in 96 games. ... The club regresses, its record dipping to 61-93 in

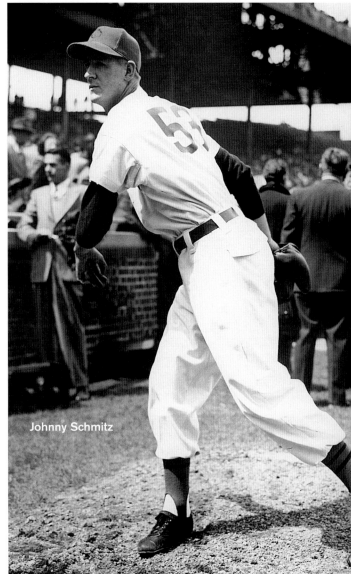

Johnny Schmitz

another basement finish. ... **Mordecai "Three Finger" Brown** is elected to the Baseball Hall of Fame.

1950

Sauer hits three successive homers off the Phillies' **Curt Simmons** as Chicago prevails, 7-5, in the first game of an August 28 doubleheader at Wrigley Field. ... Pafko (36 home runs, 92 runs batted in) and Sauer (32 homers, 103 RBIs) put a charge in the Cubs' offense, which also gets 21 homers and 85 RBIs from shortstop **Roy Smalley**. Still, the team bats a league-low .248. ... Righthander **Bob Rush** becomes the first Cub since **Phil Douglas** in 1917 to lose 20 games. ... Chicago escapes the cellar (64-89 record, seventh place).

1951

First baseman Cavarretta succeeds Frisch as manager on July 21. The Cubs are 35-45. ... A four-for-four trade on June 15 sends the popular Pafko to Brooklyn. Coming from the Dodgers are outfielder **Gene Hermanski**, infielder **Eddie Miksis**, catcher **Bruce Edwards** and pitcher **Joe Hatten**. ... In a July 29 doubleheader against the Phillies at Wrigley Field, Cavarretta shows the way. In the opener, he ties the game with an eighth-inning fly ball and drives in three

Ralph Kiner

runs overall as the Cubs win, 5-4. In the nightcap, Cavarretta breaks a 4-4 deadlock with a pinch grand slam off **Robin Roberts** in the seventh inning and Chicago goes on to win, 8-6. ... Sauer hits 30 home runs. Third baseman **Randy Jackson** adds 16 homers in his first full season with the club. ... The Cubs lose 32 of their final 45 games, finish last at 62-92.

1952

The Cubs move their spring training base from Catalina Island to Mesa, Ariz. (After spending 14 years in Mesa, one in Long Beach, Calif., and 12 in Scottsdale, Ariz., the

Cubs will begin a still-uninterrupted run in Mesa 1979.) ... Although playing on a fifth-place team that finishes 77-77, Sauer is the league's Most Valuable Player after pacing the N.L. with 121 RBIs and tying for the homer lead with 37. He is the first major leaguer to win MVP honors while playing on a club with a non-winning record. ... Baumholtz hits .325, finishes second to St. Louis' **Stan Musial** in the batting race. ... On June 11 in Chicago, Sauer has his second three-homer game against the Phils' Simmons. This time, he accounts for all of the Cubs' runs in a 3-2 triumph. ... Trailing Cincinnati by an 8-2 score

with two out and no one on base in the ninth inning of the opener of a June 29 doubleheader at Crosley Field, the Cubs erupt for seven runs and stun the Reds, 9-8. Pinch hitter **John Pramesa**'s two-run single caps the rally. ... Rush is the winning pitcher and Sauer hits a game-winning home run in the rain-shortened All-Star Game in Philadelphia. ... Rush goes 17-13 and **Warren Hacker** is 15-9. ... Hacker is second in the N.L. in ERA with his 2.58.

1953

In a June trade involving 10 players, **Ralph Kiner** is acquired from the

Pirates. ... Kiner hits 28 homers in 117 games with the Cubs. ... Injuries hamper Sauer, who plays in only 108 games and finishes with 19 home runs. ... **Ernie Banks**, a promising shortstop with the storied Kansas City Monarchs franchise of the Negro leagues, signs with the Cubs. He breaks the franchise color barrier in his big-league debut on September 17 at Wrigley Field against the Phillies, going 0-for-3 and making an error. ... On September 20 in St. Louis, Banks slugs his first major league home run, connecting against **Gerry Staley**. Another black player, second baseman **Gene Baker**, makes his debut in this game. He had been called up from Class AAA Los Angeles. ... The Cubs skid to a 65-89 record and seventh place.

1954

During spring training, Cavarretta gives a negative assessment of his team's chances and loses his job because of what ownership calls a defeatist attitude. Hack, manager of the Cubs' Los Angeles affiliate, takes over. ... The Cubs bang out 16 hits on opening day and thump the Cardinals, 13-4. They then collect 20 hits twice in their next five games, one of the sprees coming in a 23-13 triumph over the Cardinals. ... An 11-game losing streak in June sets the tone for the season, though. ... Sauer cracks 41 home runs and drives in 103 runs. ...

Banks, who had played in only 10 games in 1953, settles in as a regular and contributes 19 homers. ... Cavarretta proves prescient—the Cubs go 64-90 and again finish seventh.

1955

The Cubs' **Sam Jones** becomes the first black pitcher in major league history to pitch a no-hitter. He accomplishes the feat in dramatic fashion in a May 12 game against Pittsburgh, walking the bases loaded in the ninth inning and then striking out **Dick Groat**, rookie **Roberto Clemente** and **Frank Thomas**. The Cubs win, 4-0, at Wrigley Field. ... After games of July 4, Chicago is a surprising 44-36 and in second place, 12½ games behind Brooklyn. ... Banks sets a major league record with five grand slams. In a breakout season, he hits 44 homers overall and drives in 117 runs. ... Four Cubs—Banks, Baker, Jackson and Jones—play in the All-Star Game. ... Jones winds up losing 20 games for the Cubs, who

Bob Scheffing and the Cubs didn't earn their stripes in 1957.

falter to 72-81 (sixth place). ... **Gabby Hartnett** is elected to the Baseball Hall of Fame.

1956

After dealing away Sauer (Cardinals), Baumholtz (Phillies) and Jackson (Dodgers), the Cubs pin their hopes on newcomers. One of them, outfielder **Walt Moryn**, hits 23 homers, but the Cubs crash-land into last place with a 60-94 record. ... Banks leads the team in batting average (.297), homers (28) and RBIs (85).

1957

The Cubs have that championship look—they introduce pinstriped home uniforms. ... They also have a new manager, **Bob Scheffing**. ... More favorites depart, with Baker and first baseman **Dee Fondy** (twice a .300 hitter for the Cubs) going to the Pirates on May 1 in a trade for first baseman **Dale Long** and outfielder **Lee**

CHARLES LEO (GABBY) HARTNETT
CHICAGO N.L. 1922 TO 1940
NEW YORK N.L. 1941
CAUGHT 100 OR MORE GAMES PER SEASON
FOR 12 YEARS, EIGHT IN SUCCESSION, 1930
TO 1937 FOR LEAGUE RECORD. SET MARK
FOR CONSECUTIVE CHANCES FOR CATCHER
WITHOUT ERROR, 452 IN 1933-34. HIGHEST
FIELDING AVERAGE FOR CATCHER IN 100 OR
MORE GAMES IN 7 SEASONS; MOST PUTOUTS
N.L. 7292; MOST CHANCES ACCEPTED N.L.
8546. LIFETIME BATTING AVERAGE .297.

Walls. ... On May 26, rookie righthander **Dick Drott** strikes out 15 Milwaukee hitters in a 7-5 victory over the Braves. ... Drott goes on to post a 15-11 record. ... Walls hits for the cycle in a 10-inning game against Cincinnati on July 2. ... Righthander **Moe Drabowsky**, signed to a bonus contract in 1956, wins 13 games. ... Banks connects for 43 homers, drives in 102 runs. ... Despite the pinstripes and the standout young pitchers, it's another long season (62-92 record, a tie for seventh place). ... **Joe McCarthy** is elected to the Baseball Hall of Fame.

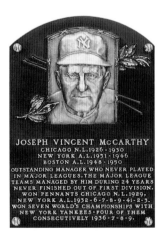

JOSEPH VINCENT McCARTHY
CHICAGO N.L. 1926 - 1930
NEW YORK A.L. 1931 - 1946
BOSTON A.L. 1948 - 1950
OUTSTANDING MANAGER WHO NEVER PLAYED
IN MAJOR LEAGUES. THE MAJOR LEAGUE
TEAMS MANAGED BY HIM DURING 24 YEARS
NEVER FINISHED OUT OF FIRST DIVISION.
WON PENNANTS CHICAGO N.L. 1929,
NEW YORK A.L. 1932 - 6 - 7 - 8 - 9 - 41 - 2 - 3.
WON SEVEN WORLD'S CHAMPIONSHIPS WITH
NEW YORK YANKEES · FOUR OF THEM
CONSECUTIVELY 1936 - 7 - 8 - 9.

In September 1953, manager Phil Cavarretta welcomed promising youngsters Gene Baker (left) and Ernie Banks to the major leagues.

Bruins Hit Bingo on Banks-Baker Combo

Rookies' Play Recalls Tinker-Evers, Jurges-Herman Acts

Pair Teamed First Time as Keystone Duo

Gene Up From Los Angeles, Ernie From Monarchs of Negro American League

By EDGAR MUNZEL

CHICAGO, Ill.

It was a gloomy Monday for the Cubs on September 14, 1953. They were in seventh place with no hope of improving their position with only two weeks left of the season, which had been one bitter disappointment after another.

But in the years to come that date may prove to be one of the brightest in the annals of the Chicago National League club.

It was on that day that two slender young Negroes reported to the Cubs. They were the first of their race to play in a Cub uniform. But that may soon be just incidental.

What will make the date of September 14, 1953, historic is that it meant the merging of a second base combination that within a short time will be etched into Cub lore alongside such keystone duos as Joe Tinker and Johnny Evers and the two Bills, Jurges and Herman.

Authority for the statement is Manager Stan Hack, who as third baseman played in the great infield of the '20s that had Jurges and Herman at its heart.

First Year as Duo

The present keystone combination consists of Ernie Banks and Gene Baker. They came from two widely divergent points. Baker reported from Los Angeles, where he had starred on the Cub farm club for three years. Banks checked in from Kansas City, where he had been playing for the Kansas City Monarchs in the Negro American League.

They had never played together before. In fact, they didn't even know each other. Neither had there been any suggestion to either that they might be ...

Couple of New Friends for Cub Flingers

[Cartoon panel]
IT'S SURE DEATH ON THE BASES WHEN THIS CUBS COMBO IS CLICKING
COULD...N YOU.! YORE.! QUIT HERE

SHORTSTOP
ERNIE BANKS, WHO HAS A WONDERFUL PAIR OF HANDS, GOBBLES UP THE BAD HOPS, TOSSES TO...

...SECOND BASEMAN GENE BAKER WHO HAS DEVELOPED INTO STEADY PERFORMER AT KEYSTONE AFTER COMING UP AS A SHORTSTOP

...asked me to come out mornings for special practice at second base. Bob Ramazzotti was assigned to teach me how to play the position. He and Coaches Roy Johnson and Ray Blades...

Called Strikes on Outside

Puzzle '.270 Hitter' Banks

Both Former Short Fielders by Profession

But Baker, Shifted to Second Base, Has Made Amazing Progress at That Position

...to make the switch to second base easier."

The next question, of course, concerns their hitting possibilities.

Banks lifted his average to .209 with an eight-game streak through May 18 in which he collected 14 hits in 32 times at bat. Baker, at the same point, was batting .219 and had replaced Ralph Kiner in the No. 3 slot because of his speed and ability to hit to right field. Certainly both seem to indicate that they will hit enough to hang onto their jobs.

"I believe Baker is one of the best two-strike hitters I've ever seen," said Cavarretta, before he was dismissed as manager. "The average batter is duck soup for the pitcher after he has two strikes on him. But Baker gets just that much tougher. Then he really bears down."

Banks' main characteristic as a batter is his wonderful wrist action.

"I believe he has about the fastest wrists I've ever seen," said Ralph Kiner, who is a student of hitting.

Baker, at 28, is five years older than Banks. They are very similar in build. Both are slender and stand six feet, one inch, though Ernie is slightly more muscular and weighs 180 to Gene's 170.

Holds Bat High Like Kiner

At the plate, Banks stands fairly straight with his bat held high, somewhat in the manner of Kiner, Baker uses a fairly deep crouch. He says he started hitting that way in the Puerto Rican Winter League a year ago and found he could follow the ball better.

Neither of them played high school baseball. They didn't have a baseball team at Booker T. Washington High in Dallas, where Banks attended, and Baker just wasn't interested in baseball at Davenport, Ia.

The top sport for ...

...be a helluva shortstop to beat out Baker. I believe Gene was as good a shortstop as I've ever seen—and that includes Pee Wee Reese."

Banks has a wonderful pair of hands.

1958

On April 24, Walls hits three home runs over the inviting left field screen at the Los Angeles Memorial Coliseum—the barrier is 251 feet from home plate—and drives in eight runs in a 15-2 win over the Dodgers, who had moved from Brooklyn to the West Coast after the 1957 season. ... Three weeks into the schedule, the Cubs are 13-7 and sit

Ron Santo

Cubs catcher **Sammy Taylor** thinks the pitch nicks Musial's bat–and the home-plate umpire gives Anderson another. Both balls are pegged to second base in an attempt to nail the in-flight Musial, who tries to reach third when one ball sails into the outfield. When everything is sorted out, Musial, tagged by shortstop Banks, is called out. ... Major league baseball sanctions interleague trading, and the Cubs and Red Sox make the first deal. On November 21, the Cubs trade pitcher **Dave Hillman** and outfielder **Jim Marshall** to Boston for first baseman **Dick Gernert**.

1960

Grimm returns as Cubs manager but his stay is short-lived. On May 4, with Chicago owning a 6-11 record, Grimm and Cubs broadcaster **Lou Boudreau** switch jobs. ... Righthander **Don Cardwell** is obtained in a May 13 trade with the Phillies. In his first start for Chicago, Cardwell throws a no-hitter against the Cardinals on May 15. The 4-0 gem comes in the second game of a doubleheader at Wrigley Field and is preserved by left fielder Moryn's sensational two-out catch in the ninth inning. ... The Cubs summon **Ron Santo** from their Class AAA Houston farm club in late June. Santo, 20, is installed as the regular third baseman. ... Chicago, 60-94, dips to

atop the N.L. standings. They then lose seven consecutive games. ... Chicago is 45-41 on July 16 but goes into a tailspin and never recovers. ... Banks becomes the first player on a losing team to win MVP honors in the majors. Playing for a 72-82 Cubs team that ties for fifth place, he leads the N.L. with 129 RBIs and a career-high 47 home runs.

... Long, a lefthanded thrower, appears in two games as a catcher.

1959

Banks repeats as the league MVP. He has a career-best and N.L.-leading 143 RBIs and drills 45 homers for a Cubs team that finishes in a fifth-place deadlock at 74-80. ... **Glen Hobbie** compiles a

16-13 record and **Bob Anderson** wins 12 games. ... Cubs relievers **Don Elston** and **Bill Henry** share the league record for most appearances with 65. ... In a June 30 game against St. Louis at Wrigley Field, two balls are in play at the same time. One ball, at first unattended, rolls to the screen–it is ball four to the Cardinals' Musial but

Buck O'Neil

seventh place. ... Banks leads the N.L. with 41 homers. ... Hobbie again wins 16 games despite absorbing 20 losses. ... **Sammy Drake**'s pinch-running appearance for the Cubs in an early-season game makes Sammy and **Solly Drake** (a 1956 Cub) the first black brothers in modern major league baseball.

1961

Frustrated that the team hadn't recorded a winning season since 1946, Cubs officials eliminate the position of full-time manager and implement a rotating "College of Coaches" system. **Elvin Tappe** sees the longest tenure as the No. 1 coach, but **Vedie Himsl**, **Harry Craft** and **Lou Klein** also serve in that capacity. ... The Cubs go 64-90 (seventh place). ... Left fielder **Billy Williams** hits 25 homers and drives in 86 runs and is voted the league's Rookie of the Year. ... Fleet

outfielder **Lou Brock** is one of the late-season call-ups. He had spent the year with St. Cloud of the Class C Northern League.

1962

The New York Mets and Houston Colt .45s join the National League as expansion teams, boosting the N.L. membership to 10 teams. The schedule is expanded from 154 games to 162. ... **Charlie Metro** heads the coaching rotation. ... The Cubs make **Buck O'Neil** the first black coach in big-league history. O'Neil had been a longtime player and manager in the Negro leagues. ... Banks is moved from shortstop to first base, with **Andre Rodgers** taking over at short. ... **Ken Hubbs** is named the N.L. Rookie of the Year. He sets major league records for a second baseman for consecutive errorless games (78) and consecutive errorless chances (418) during a

season in which he hits .260 for the Cubs. ... Outfielder **George Altman** bats .318. ... Chicago posts a dismal 59-103 record, its worst ever, but still finishes ninth, 18 games ahead of the last-place Mets. ... Lefthander **Dick Ellsworth** is a 20-game loser. ... Capping a four-year period in which two All-Star Games were played each season, the A.L. wins the second game of 1962 by a 9-4 score on July 30 at Wrigley Field. The Cubs' Banks, Williams and Altman appear in the game.

1963

The rotating-coaches system ends. **Bob Kennedy** is "head coach" for the entire season. ... With the Cubs trailing Houston, 5-2, in the bottom of the ninth inning of an August 31 game at Wrigley Field, center fielder **Ellis Burton** hits a two-out, game-winning grand slam. ... The Cubs make a dramatic improvement in their won-lost record, going 82-80. Their first winning season in 17 years is good for only a seventh-place finish, though. ... Santo ties Williams for the team

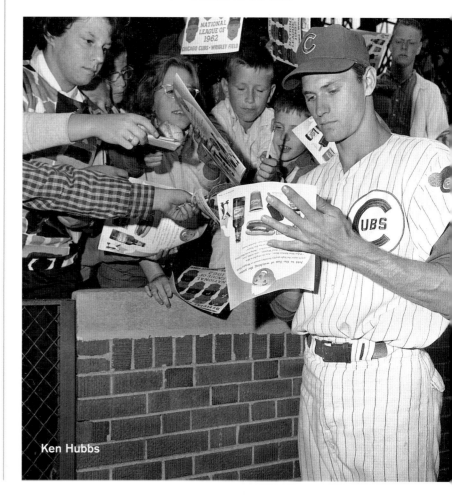
Ken Hubbs

homer lead with 25 and tops the club in RBIs with 99. ... Ellsworth does an amazing turnabout—he wins 22 games. ... **John Clarkson** is elected to the Baseball Hall of Fame.

1964

In February, Hubbs, 22, is killed in the crash of his light plane in Utah. ... The sixth-place Cubs, 27-27, obtain pitcher **Ernie Broglio** in a June 15 trade with the Cardinals, who are tied for seventh at 28-30. Broglio had won 18 games for the Cards in 1963 and 21 for St. Louis in 1960. Chicago gives up promising outfielder Brock in the six-player deal. ... Broglio goes 4-7 for the Cubs the rest of the season. Brock hits .348 for the Cardinals and helps his new team to the pennant and World Series title. ... Righthander **Larry Jackson**, obtained from the Cardinals in October 1962, compiles a 24-11 record. His victory total is the highest by a Cub in 37 years. ... Santo and Williams combine for 63 homers and 212 RBIs. ...

The Cubs finish in eighth place with a 76-86 record.

1965

Cubs broadcaster **Jack Quinlan** is killed in an automobile accident near the team's Arizona spring-training site. ... In June, Kennedy is replaced as manager by Klein. ... Alabama high school pitcher **Rick James** is the Cubs' No. 1 pick in baseball's first amateur draft. ... On July 22, Cubs catcher **Ed Bailey** belts a grand slam and a three-run homer in a 4-for-4, eight-RBI spree. The Phillies fall, 10-6. ... Cincinnati's **Jim Maloney** pitches a 10-inning no-hitter against the Cubs on August 19. ... The Dodgers' **Sandy Koufax** hurls a perfect game against Chicago on September 9. The Cubs' **Bob Hendley** gives up

only one hit but winds up a 1-0 loser. (Through the 2004 season, Koufax's gem marks the last time the Cubs have been victimized by a no-hitter.) ... The Cubs turn three triple plays during the season—all while **Bill Faul** is pitching for Chicago. ... Williams (34 homers, 108 RBIs), Santo (33, 101) and Banks (28, 106) put up impressive power numbers. ... Jackson loses 21 games. ... The Cubs' 72-90 record leaves them in eighth place.

1966

Leo Durocher, who had last managed in the majors in 1955, takes over as Cubs manager. ... In a June 11 game at Houston, Banks ties a modern major league record with three triples in an 8-2 Chicago triumph. In the same game, Cubs center

fielder **Adolfo Phillips** strikes out for the ninth consecutive time. ... Durocher endures a long season as his team loses 103 games, matching 1962's futility, and finishes last. ... The Cubs acquire righthander **Ferguson Jenkins** from the Phillies in an April trade. ... Santo leads the club in home runs (30) and RBIs (94). ... Ellsworth loses 22 games.

1967

In a stunning turn-around, the Cubs rise to third place with an 87-74 record. ... On June 11, Phillips is the headliner in a doubleheader sweep of the Mets. He hits a solo home run in the opener, then goes on a three-homer, seven-RBI tear in the nightcap. ... Starting on June 20, the Cubs win

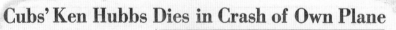

The deaths in successive years of second baseman Ken Hubbs in a plane crash and broadcaster Jack Quinlan in an car accident stunned the Cubs and their fans.

14 of 15 games and move into a first-place tie with St. Louis. They then lose seven straight preceding the All-Star Game break. ... Jenkins helps fuel the season reversal with a 20-victory season. ... Military duty limits **Ken Holtzman** to 12 starts, but the young lefthander makes the most of his abbreviated season. He compiles a 9-0 record and a 2.53 ERA. ... Santo, Banks and Williams combine for 82 homers and 277 runs batted in. ... Phillips hits 17 home runs and catcher **Randy Hundley** contributes 14. ... The Cubs' first-ever draft pick, righthander James, reaches the majors at age 19. He appears in three games for the Cubs and goes 0-1 with a 13.50 ERA. He never again pitches in the big leagues.

1968

Jenkins again wins 20 games for the Cubs, who repeat as third-place finishers with an 84-78 record. ... Righthanders **Bill Hands** and **Joe Niekro** combine for 30 victories. ... **Phil Regan** makes 68 relief appearances for the Cubs, going 10-5 with a 2.20 ERA and 25 saves (which are a year away from being an official statistic). ... Banks (32 home runs, 83 RBIs), Santo (26, 98) and Williams (30, 98) continue their heavy hitting. ... Santo wins his fifth consecutive Gold Glove. ... **Kiki Cuyler** is elected to the Baseball Hall of Fame.

HAZEN SHIRLEY CUYLER
"KIKI"

PITTSBURGH N.L. 1921 TO 1927
CHICAGO N.L. 1928 TO 1935
CINCINNATI N.L. 1935 TO 1937
BROOKLYN N.L. 1938
LED N.L. IN STOLEN BASES 1926, 1928, 1929, 1930. BATTED .354 IN 1924, .357 IN 1925, .360 IN 1929, .355 IN 1930. LIFETIME TOTAL 2299 HITS, BATTING AVERAGE .321, NAMED TO ALL STAR TEAM IN 1925.

1969

The major leagues expand by four teams and adopt divisional play. ... In the season opener, the Cubs defeat the Phillies, 7-6, at Wrigley Field on pinch hitter **Willie Smith**'s two-run homer in the 11th inning. ... Durocher's Cubs get off to an 11-1 start. ... Entering a July 8-9-10 series at Shea Stadium, the Cubs lead New York by five games in the N.L. East. Center fielder **Don Young** mishandles two fly balls in the ninth inning of the first game, helping the Mets rally from a 3-1 deficit to a 4-3 victory. **Tom Seaver** then comes within two outs of a perfect game—**Jim Qualls**' single ruins his bid—in a 4-0 New York triumph. But the Cubs rebound, winning nine of their next 14 games. ... On August 14, Chicago is $8\frac{1}{2}$ games ahead of the Cardinals and $9\frac{1}{2}$ in front of the Mets in the division race. But from September 3 through September 15, the Cubs lose eight consecutive games and 11 of 12. They fall out of first place on September 10 and never regain the lead as the Mets win the East by eight games over second-place Chicago (92-70). ... Particularly tough losses occur on September 7 and 8. In the first of those games, the Cubs lead the Pirates, 5-4, with two out in the ninth inning at Wrigley Field when **Willie Stargell** homers off Regan. Pittsburgh goes

Righthander Joe Niekro (left) went 10-7 for the Cubs in 1967 and 14-10 in 1968 but was dealt to San Diego in April 1969 in a trade that brought Dick Selma to Chicago.

on to win, 7-5, in 11 innings. The next night, the Cubs lose, 3-2, at Shea Stadium, on a disputed sixth-inning call at home plate. The Cubs think right fielder **Jim Hickman**'s throw to the plate nails the Mets' **Tommie Agee** (who had raced home on **Wayne Garrett**'s single). The umpire thinks otherwise. ... A black cat strolls past the Cubs' dugout during a 7-1 loss on September 9 at Shea. ... Santo, Banks, Williams and Hickman hit more than 20 homers and catcher **Randy Hundley** connects for 18. ... The season is Banks' last as an everyday player. ... Jenkins goes 21-15, Hands 20-14 and Holtzman 17-13. ... Holtzman throws a no-hitter against Atlanta on August 19.

The appearance of a black cat near the Cubs' dugout at Shea Stadium was not exactly the kind of omen the team was looking for in 1969.

two-run homer. ... Just 1½ games behind the division-leading Pirates on September 19, Chicago loses seven of its next nine games and falls out of contention. ... The Cubs finish second in the N.L. East at 84-78. ... Williams is fourth in the league in hitting (.322), second in home runs (42) and second (tie) in RBIs (129). He also extends his National League record for consecutive games played to 1,117 before sitting out a September game. ... Hickman (115) and Santo (114) also reach the 100-RBI plateau. ... Jenkins, Hands and Holtzman win 22, 18 and 17 games, respectively. ... Shortstop **Don Kessinger**, a regular since 1965, earns his second straight Gold Glove.

1970

On May 12, Banks hits his 500th career home run. He connects off Atlanta's **Pat Jarvis** at Wrigley Field. Banks is the ninth player to reach the milestone in major league history. ... The Cubs, who had an 11-game winning streak in April, are in first place on June 20 with a 35-25 record. They drop their next 12 games. ... On July 6, Santo hits a grand slam and a three-run home run and drives in eight runs in the second game of a doubleheader against Montreal. In the opener, he connects for a decisive

1971

Holtzman pitches his second career no-hitter, baffling the Reds on June 3 in Cincinnati. ... Kessinger goes 6-for-6 and scores the winning

run in a 10-inning victory over the Cardinals on June 17 in Chicago. ... Jenkins compiles a 24-13 record, pitches 30 complete games and has a 2.77 ERA. ... **Milt Pappas** is 17-14, but Hands (12-18) and Holtzman (9-15) struggle. ... Second baseman **Glenn Beckert**, a steady hitter over the previous five seasons (.287, .280, .294, .291, .288), bats an eye-popping .342. ... Banks ends his playing career, hitting three homers in 39 games. ... The 83-79 Cubs tie for third place.

1972

A players strike forces a delay in the start of the major league season and the cancellation of 86 games overall. ... Durocher begins his seventh year at the Cubs' helm. ... Cubs righthander **Burt Hooton**, making only his fourth start in the majors, hurls a no-hitter in the team's second game of the season. His gem comes against

the Phillies on April 16 at Wrigley Field. ... With the Cubs' record at 46-44, Durocher is replaced by **Whitey Lockman** on the eve of the All-Star Game.

Whitey Lockman

... Pappas misses a perfect game on September 2 at Wrigley Field when he walks Padres pinch hitter **Larry Stahl** on a 3-2 pitch with two out in the ninth inning. He retires the next batter, completing the Cubs' fourth no-hitter in the past four seasons. ... The club does well under Lockman, forging a 39-26 record, but Chicago finishes second its 85-70 record, 11 games back. ... Williams hits an N.L.-leading .333. He has 37 homers and 122 RBIs. ... Jenkins is 20-12 and Pappas goes 17-7. Hooton winds up 11-14.

Burt Hooton

Rick
Monday

1974

Catcher **George Mitterwald** hits three homers, one a grand slam, and has eight RBIs as the Cubs rout the Pirates, 18-9, on April 17. ... With the team's record at 41-52 three weeks into July, Cubs coach **Jim Marshall** takes over for Lockman. ... Promising third baseman **Bill Madlock**, obtained the previous October in a swap that sent Jenkins to Texas, hits .313. ... **Bill Bonham** goes 11-22. It is the sixth time in 20 seasons that a Cubs pitcher loses 20 games. ...

Chicago sinks to the basement with a 66-96 record. ... In October, Williams is dealt to Oakland.

1975

Madlock goes 6-for-6 against the Mets on July 26, but the Cubs lose, 9-8, in 10 innings at Wrigley Field. ... On August 21, Reuschel and brother Paul combine to shut out the Dodgers, 7-0, at Wrigley. Rick allows five hits in $6\frac{1}{3}$ innings, Paul one in $2\frac{2}{3}$ innings. ... Madlock goes on to win the N.L. batting crown with a mark of .354. ... In

1973

In late June, the Cubs are 47-31 and atop the division by $8\frac{1}{2}$ games. They skid to fifth place (77-84) in the six-team N.L. East. ... Center fielder **Rick Monday** cracks 26 home runs, and right fielder **Jose Cardenal** bats .303. ... Rotation mainstays Jenkins, Hooton, Pappas and **Rick Reuschel** all have losing records. ... In December, Santo is traded to the White Sox in a deal that sends righthander **Steve Stone** and three other players to the North Side.

Steve
Stone

George
Mitterwald

the biggest shutout rout to date in major league history, the Cubs suffer a 22-0 pounding at the hands of the Pirates. (The Yankees lose by the same score in 2004.) Pittsburgh's **Rennie Stennett** goes 7-for-7 in the September 16 embarrassment at Wrigley Field. ... Chicago ties for fifth place with a 75-87 record. ... **Billy Herman** is elected to the Baseball Hall of Fame.

WILLIAM JENNINGS HERMAN
CHICAGO, N. L.   BROOKLYN, N. L.
BOSTON, N. L.   PITTSBURGH, N. L.
1931 – 1947
MASTER OF HIT-AND-RUN PLAY OWNED .304
LIFETIME BATTING AVERAGE. MADE 200 OR
MORE HITS IN SEASON THREE TIMES. LED
LEAGUE IN HITS (227) AND DOUBLES (57)
IN 1935. SET MAJOR LEAGUE RECORD FOR
SECOND BASEMEN WITH FIVE SEASONS OF
HANDLING 900 OR MORE CHANCES AND N.L.
MARK OF 466 PUTOUTS IN 1933. LED LOOP
KEYSTONERS IN PUTOUTS SEVEN TIMES.

1976

In an April 17 game at Wrigley Field, the Phillies' **Mike Schmidt** smashes four home runs and a single as the Cubs fall, 18-16, in 10 innings. Chicago had led, 12-1, after three innings. ... On April 25 at Dodger Stadium, Monday snatches an American flag from two persons who have run onto the field and apparently are about to set the flag on fire. ... Cardenal's sixth hit of the game, a 14th-inning single, drives in the winning run in the first game of a May 2 doubleheader at San Francisco. ... Madlock

repeats as the league batting champion, this time hitting .339. ... Monday has 32 homers. ... **Ray Burris** wins 15 games for the second year in a row. ... Chicago matches its won-lost mark of the previous season, finishing fourth this time.

1977

P.K. Wrigley, owner of the club since 1932, dies. Principal interest in the Cubs is left to son **William Wrigley**. ... Outfielder

Bobby Murcer

Bobby Murcer, obtained in a trade that sent Madlock

ERNEST BANKS
"MR. CUB"
CHICAGO N. L., 1953-1971
HIT 512 CAREER HOMERS WITH MORE THAN
40 IN A SEASON FIVE TIMES. HAD RECORD
FIVE GRAND-SLAMS IN 1955. FIRST TO BE
ELECTED N.L. MOST VALUABLE PLAYER TWO
SUCCESSIVE YEARS, 1958-59. LED LEAGUE
IN HOME RUNS AND RUNS BATTED IN TWICE
AND SLUGGING PCT. ONCE. ESTABLISHED
RECORDS FOR MOST HOMERS IN SEASON BY
SHORTSTOP (47 IN 1958) AND FOR FEWEST
ERRORS (12) AND BEST FIELDING AVERAGE
(.985) BY A SHORTSTOP IN 1959.

to the Giants, hits 27 home runs for the Cubs, now managed by **Herman Franks**. ... Reuschel wins 20 games, tosses four shutouts and has a 2.79 ERA. ... **Bruce Sutter**, in his first full season in the major leagues, saves 31 games and records a 1.35 ERA despite shoulder problems. ... Franks' team goes 81-81 (fourth place) after being 25 games over .500 at one point. ... **Ernie Banks** is elected to the Baseball Hall of Fame.

Dick Tidrow

LEWIS ROBERT WILSON
"HACK"
NEW YORK N.L., CHICAGO N.L.,
BROOKLYN N.L., PHILADELPHIA N.L.,
1923-1934
ESTABLISHED MAJOR LEAGUE RECORD OF 190
RUNS BATTED IN AND NATIONAL LEAGUE HIGH
OF 56 HOMERS IN 1930. LED OR TIED FOR N.L.
HOMER TITLE FOUR TIMES. COMPILED LIFETIME
.307 BATTING AVERAGE AND DROVE IN 100 OR
MORE RUNS SIX YEARS. HIT TWO HOMERS IN
INNING IN 1925 AND THREE IN GAME IN 1930.

saves. ... Reuschel is 18-12. ... **Hack Wilson** is elected to the Baseball Hall of Fame. ... **Bob Elson**, noted Cubs announcer from 1928-41, is elected to the broadcasters wing of the Baseball Hall of Fame.

1980

Dodgers coach **Preston Gomez** becomes Chicago manager. ... Catcher **Barry Foote**'s bases-empty homer in the eighth inning ties the game and his grand slam with two out in the ninth inning wins it as the Cubs outslug St. Louis, 16-12, on April 22. Foote has an eight-RBI

Barry Foote

1978

Free-agent outfielder **Dave Kingman** joins the Cubs and hits 28 home runs. Three of his homers come in a May 14 victory over the Dodgers, with his three-run shot in the 15th inning deciding the 10-7 game. Kingman, who finishes with eight RBIs, had tied the game with a two-out, two-run homer in the ninth. ... First baseman

Bill Buckner, acquired in January 1977 in a trade that sent Monday to the Dodgers, bats .323. ... Sutter saves 27 games for a 79-83 team that winds up third in the East Division.

1979

The Cubs and Phillies play a 45-run game on May 17. The Cubs trail, 21-9, after 4½ innings,

rally for a 22-22 tie and then lose when the Phils score a run in the 10th inning. Buckner drives in seven runs for Chicago, and Kingman has three home runs and six RBIs for the Cubs. ... Franks gives way to coach **Joe Amalfitano** in the final week. ... The club wins 80, loses 82 and finishes fifth. ... Kingman's 48 homers lead the league. ... Sutter tops the N.L. with 37

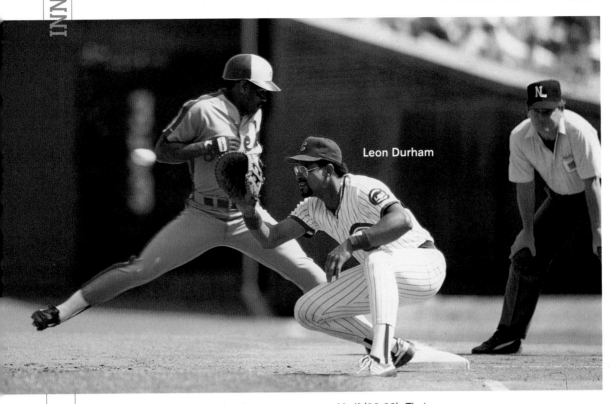

Leon Durham

1982

Lee Elia, a Phillies coach in 1980 and 1981, is the Cubs' new manager. ... Jenkins returns to the club as a free agent. ... **Harry Caray** joins the Cubs' broadcast team. ... On January 27, the Cubs deal shortstop **Ivan DeJesus** to the Phillies for shortstop **Larry Bowa** and infielder **Ryne Sandberg**. ... Sandberg, who played primarily at shortstop in the minors in 1981, becomes the Cubs' third baseman. ... Jenkins records his 3,000th career strikeout, fanning the Padres' **Garry Templeton** in the third inning of a May 25 game in San Diego. ... A 7-0 loss to **Fernando Valenzuela**

day. ... Buckner wins the N.L. batting crown with a .324 mark. ... Sutter paces N.L. closers with 28 saves. ... Reliever **Dick Tidrow** appears in a league-high 84 games. ... The Cubs are a huge disappointment, collapsing to a 64-98 record and last place. ... Coach Amalfitano again winds up as manager, succeeding Gomez with the Cubs' record at 38-52. ... In December, Sutter is traded to the Cardinals for outfielder/first baseman **Leon "Bull" Durham**, third baseman **Ken Reitz** and infielder/outfielder **Ty Waller.**

1981

A players strike results in a shortened, split season. Amalfitano's Cubs finish last in the first half (15-37) and fifth in the

second half (23-28). Their overall record of 38-65 is worst in the N.L. East. ... In June, the Wrigley family announces the sale of the Cubs franchise to the Tribune Company. ... **Dallas Green**, who had managed the Phillies to the World Series championship in 1980, is named Cubs general manager in October.

The Wrigley family gave baseball something to chew on when it gave up ownership of the Cubs in June 1981.

Dallas Green

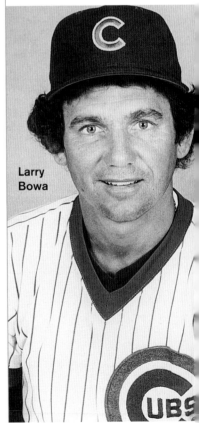

Larry Bowa

and the Dodgers on May 30 marks the beginning of a 13-game losing streak. ... Buckner drives in 105 runs. ... Durham hits 22 homers. ... **Lee Smith** appears in 72 games and notches 17 saves. ... Chicago finishes fifth at 73-89.

1983

Sandberg moves to second base. ... Irate over what he terms unfair criticism from Cubs fans, Elia goes into an expletive-filled tirade against those fans in an early-season news conference. ... With the Cubs in fifth place, Elia loses his job on August 22. **Charlie Fox** replaces him. ... Third baseman **Ron Cey**, acquired in a trade with the Dodgers, and catcher **Jody Davis** each hit 24 home runs for the fifth-place Cubs (71-91). ... Smith leads the league in saves with 29 and has a 1.65 ERA. ... **Jack Brickhouse**, who called Cubs games for nearly four decades, is elected to the broadcasters wing of the Baseball Hall of Fame.

1984

Jim Frey, who had managed the Royals to the 1980 American League pennant, becomes manager. ... On May 25, the Cubs bolster their rotation by acquiring **Dennis Eckersley** from the Red Sox in a deal that sends Buckner to Boston. ... In another trade to boost the pitching staff,

Jim Frey

the club obtains **Rick Sutcliffe** from Cleveland on June 13 in a six-player deal that moves promising outfield prospect **Joe Carter** to the Indians. ... Sandberg hits tying home runs off St. Louis' Sutter in the ninth and 10th innings of a June 23 game at Wrigley Field and drives in seven runs overall in an 11-inning, 12-11 triumph. Pinch hitter **Dave Owen** singles home the winning run. ... At the

Steve Trout

All-Star Game break, the Cubs are a half-game behind the N.L. East-leading Mets. ... A 12-2 run beginning on July 28 lifts Chicago into first place. ... The club wins nine of 10 games in a spurt ending September 4 and builds a seven-game lead over second-place New York. ... Sutcliffe's 14th consecutive victory—a 4-1 triumph at Pittsburgh on September 24—clinches the East Division title. It is

the Cubs' first championship since their N.L. pennant 39 years earlier. ... Sutcliffe is 16-1 as a Cub, **Steve Trout** goes 13-7 and Eckersley is 10-8. ... Smith has 33 saves. .... Six Cubs drive in 80 or more runs. Cey, Durham and Davis lead the way with 97, 96 and 94 RBIs, respectively. ... The Cubs, who finish 96-65, seize a 2-0 lead in the best-of-five N.L. Championship Series but lose three straight in San Diego. ... Sandberg (19 homers, 84 RBIs, .314 batting average and a Gold Glove) is voted the league's MVP. ... Sutcliffe wins the N.L. Cy Young Award. ... Center fielder **Bob Dernier** also earns a Gold Glove. ... Frey is chosen N.L. Manager of the Year. ... Cubs attendance tops two million for the first time, totaling 2,107,655.

1985

The Cubs get off to a 7-1 start in defense of their N.L. East title. ... Leading the division with a 35-19 record on June 11, Frey's team loses 13 consecutive games and drops to fourth place. ... Cincinnati's **Pete Rose** ties **Ty Cobb**'s all-time hits record by collecting Nos. 4,189, 4,190 and 4,191 against the Cubs' **Reggie Patterson** in a September series at

Wrigley Field. ... Injuries take a toll. Sutcliffe has three stints on the disabled list, and fellow starters Eckersley, Trout, **Scott Sanderson** and **Dick Ruthven** also have lengthy stays on the D.L. ... At season's end, the Cubs are 23½ games out of first place. They are fourth with a 77-84 record. ... Seven Cubs have double-figure homer totals. ... Right fielder **Keith Moreland**, who hits 14 home runs, drives in 106 runs. ... Smith records 33 saves.

Gene Michael

1986

With the club off to a 23-33 start, Frey and coach **Don Zimmer** are dismissed. Green hires Yankees coach **Gene Michael** as manager. ... Shortstop **Shawon Dunston**, in his first full season as a regular, hits 17 homers. ... Sutcliffe and Eckersley finish a

Andre
Dawson

BILLY LEO WILLIAMS
CHICAGO, N.L., 1959 - 1974
OAKLAND, A.L., 1975 - 1976
SOFT-SPOKEN, CLUTCH PERFORMER. WAS ONE OF
MOST RESPECTED HITTERS OF HIS DAY. BATTED SOLID
.290 OVER 18 SEASONS SOCKING 426 HOME RUNS. HIT 20
OR MORE HOMERS 13 STRAIGHT SEASONS. 1961 N.L.
ROOKIE OF YEAR. 1972 N.L. BATTING CHAMPION WITH
.333. HELD N.L. RECORD FOR CONSECUTIVE GAMES
PLAYED WITH 1117.

combined 11-25 as Chicago stumbles to a 70-90 record (fifth place).

1987

Andre Dawson, signed as a free agent, becomes the first player in major league history to win the MVP award while playing for a last-place team. He pounds 49 homers and drives in 137 runs (both N.L. highs) for a Cubs team that goes 76-85. ... In early September, **Frank Lucchesi** takes over for Michael. ... Moreland and Durham each hit 27 home runs. Young outfielder/first baseman **Rafael Palmeiro** contributes 14 homers in 221 at-bats. ... Sutcliffe rebounds for an 18-victory season and **Jamie Moyer** wins 12 games. ... Smith has 36 saves. ... **Billy Williams** is elected to the Baseball Hall of Fame.

1988

Zimmer, former Cubs player and coach, becomes manager. ... On February 25, the Chicago City Council clears the way for night baseball at Wrigley Field. A vote of 29-19 allows eight night games this season and 18 in future years. ...

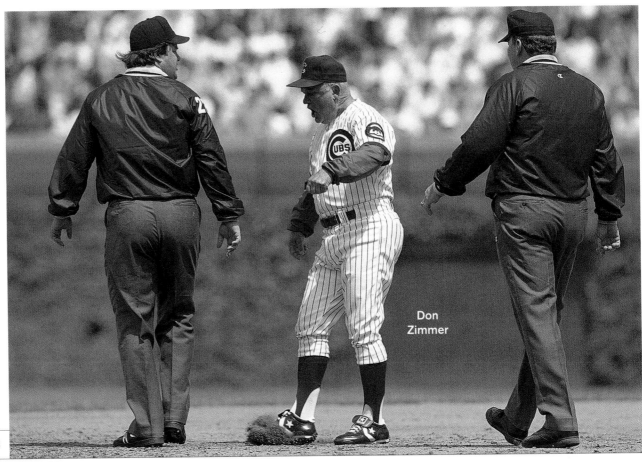

Don
Zimmer

Jeff Pico

Righthander **Jeff Pico**, making his major league debut on May 31 after being called up from Class AAA Iowa, pitches a four-hit shutout against Cincinnati. ... Night baseball, with all its attendant hoopla, comes to Wrigley on August 8—until Mother Nature intervenes. After the Cubs seize a 3-1 lead against the Phillies, the game is rained out in the bottom of the fourth inning. The next night, the Cubs and Mets play the first official under-the-lights game in Wrigley Field history. Chicago wins, 6-4. ... Pitching in his first full major league season, Cubs righthander **Greg Maddux** is 18-8 with a 3.18 ERA. ... First baseman **Mark Grace**, brought up from the minors in early May, bats .296. ... Dawson falls off to 24 homers and 79 RBIs. ... Dunston steals 30 bases. ... The Cubs are 77-85 and fourth-place finishers. ... In December, the Cubs and Rangers make a nine-player deal that ships Palmeiro and Moyer to Texas and sends reliever **Mitch Williams** to Chicago.

1989

After losing its seventh straight game on June 29, Zimmer's team goes on a 31-13 surge and moves into first place in the N.L. East. ... Newcomer **Jerome Walton** goes on a July-August hitting streak that reaches 30 games. ... In an August 29 game at Wrigley Field in which the Cubs trail Houston, 9-0, after 4½ innings, rookie **Dwight Smith** enters play in the seventh inning as a defensive replacement for right fielder Dawson. Smith singles home a run in the seventh, throws out a runner at the plate in the eighth, ties the game at 9-9 with a sacrifice fly in the Cubs' eighth and drives in the winning run in a 10-9 outcome with a 10th-inning single. ... The 93-69 Cubs win the division by six games. ... Maddux goes 19-12, **Mike Bielecki** 18-7 and Sutcliffe 16-11. ...Williams posts 36 saves. ... Sandberg slugs 30 homers. ... Center fielder Walton hits .293 and steals 24 bases. He is named N.L. Rookie of the Year. ... Zimmer is selected N.L. Manager of the Year. ... Grace bats .647

Jerome Walton

Dwight Smith

in the NLCS but the Giants prevail, four games to one. ... **Harry Caray** is elected to the broadcasters wing of the Baseball Hall of Fame.

Harry Caray

1990
The Cubs tumble to 77-85 and a tie for fourth place. ... Sandberg leads the league in homers (40), total bases (344) and runs (116). He drives in 100 runs. ... Dawson has a 27-homer, 100-RBI season. ... The staff ERA goes from 3.43 in 1989 to 4.34. ... Williams is 1-8 with only 16 saves. ... Rookie **Mike Harkey** fashions a 12-6 record. ... The All-Star Game is played at Wrigley Field for the third time, and A.L. pitchers combine for a two-hitter in a 2-0 victory. With the midsummer classic now a prime-time attraction, the Cubs are able to play host to the

game because of the installation of lights two years earlier. Sandberg and Dawson are N.L. starters, and Dunston sees reserve duty.

1991
Zimmer is fired in May amid a dispute over the Cubs' refusal to renew his contract during the season. **Jim Essian**, manager at Class AAA Iowa, succeeds him. ... Chicago nearly duplicates its 1990 record, winding up 77-83 and fourth in the N.L. East. ... Sandberg wins his ninth consecutive Gold Glove. ... Dawson, Sandberg and

FERGUSON ARTHUR JENKINS

George Bell

free-agent signee **George Bell** knock in 104, 100 and 86 runs, respectively. ... Maddux wins 15 games. ... **Ferguson Jenkins** is elected to the Baseball Hall of Fame.

1992
Jim Lefebvre, manager of the Seattle Mariners the previous three seasons, is the Cubs' new pilot. ... A

Thanks to the installation of lights two years earlier, the Cubs were able to play host to the All-Star Game in '90. Ryne Sandberg and Andre Dawson were starters for the N.L.

In March 1992, the Cubs acquired a player who at the time had 29 career homers. His name: Sammy Sosa.

week before the start of the season, the Cubs trade outfielder Bell to the White Sox for outfielder **Sammy Sosa** and pitcher **Ken Patterson**. ... Sosa hits his first home run as a Cub on May 7, connecting off Houston's **Ryan Bowen** at Wrigley Field. ... Maddux wins 20 games and has a 2.18 ERA. He wins the N.L. Cy Young Award. ... The Cubs remain consistent in the won-lost column, going 78-84 and finishing fourth. ... On December 9, Maddux and Dawson depart as free agents, Maddux signing with the Braves and Dawson joining the Red Sox. On the same day, free-agent closer **Randy Myers** becomes a Cub.

1993

The N.L. grows from 12 to 14 teams with the addition of the expansion Colorado Rockies and Florida Marlins. ... Sosa enjoys a 6-for-6 night as the Cubs down the Rockies, 11-8, on July 2 at Mile High Stadium. ... Sosa has a breakout power season with 33 homers and 93 RBIs. He also steals 36 bases. ... Grace bats .325 with 39 doubles, 14 home runs and 98 runs batted in. ... Myers sets a league record with 53 saves, which helps Lefebvre's team improve to an 84-78 mark. Still, the club again finishes fourth.

1994

The structure of major league baseball is overhauled. The leagues realign into East, West and Central divisions, and a wild-card team is added to postseason play. ... The Lefebvre managerial era lasts two seasons. **Tom Trebelhorn**, former manager of the Brewers and a Cubs coach in 1992 and 1993, takes over the team. ... In the April 4 season opener against the Mets at Wrigley Field, Chicago leadoff hitter **Karl "Tuffy" Rhodes** slams three bases-empty homers off **Dwight Gooden**. Yet Gooden and the Mets prevail, 12-8. ... With the Cubs in last place and his own game faltering (.238 batting average in 223 at-bats), Sandberg makes a surprise announcement on June 13: He's retiring, effective immediately. ... Baseball's labor negotiations are bogged down— and so are the Cubs. Trebelhorn's team is 36-50 and last in the Central Division at the All-Star Game break. ...Major league players go on strike August 12 and don't return. ... Owners cancel the World Series on September 14. ... The Cubs' final record is 49-64. They finish in the basement.

1995

Jim Riggleman, manager of the Padres since September 1992, is hired to replace Trebelhorn. ... The labor impasse is resolved in early April. With spring training delayed, the start of the season is pushed back and the schedule is reduced to 144 games. ... In an August 18 game at Coors Field in Denver, the Cubs crush Colorado, 26-7, amassing 27 hits.

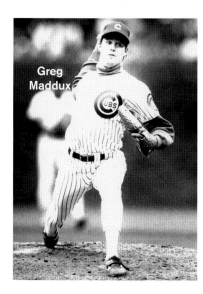

Greg Maddux

Randy Myers

Frank
Castillo

WILLIAM AMBROSE HULBERT

WAVY-HAIRED, SILVER TONGUED EXECUTIVE AND
ENERGETIC, INFLUENTIAL LEADER. WHILE PART-
OWNER OF CHICAGO NATIONAL ASSOCIATION TEAM,
WAS INSTRUMENTAL IN FOUNDING NATIONAL LEAGUE
IN 1876. ELECTED N.L. PRESIDENT LATER THAT
YEAR AND IS CREDITED WITH ESTABLISHING
RESPECTABILITY, INTEGRITY AND SOUND
FOUNDATION FOR NEW LEAGUE WITH HIS
RELENTLESS OPPOSITION TO BETTING, ROWDINESS,
AND OTHER PREVALENT ABUSES WHICH WERE
THREATENING THE SPORT

and a half. ... **William Hulbert** is elected to the Baseball Hall of Fame. A Chicago businessman, Hulbert was instrumental in the founding of the National League, became the N.L. president and helped organize (and then oversaw) the league's Chicago franchise.

1996

The Cubs (76-86) slip to fourth in the Central

Division. ... Grace (.331) again is fifth in the league in hitting. ... Sosa connects for a career-high 40 homers. ... Sandberg bats only .244 in his return, but he has a 25-homer, 92-RBI season. ... **Jaime Navarro** and **Steve Trachsel** combine for 28 wins.

1997

The Cubs set an N.L. record by losing their first 14 games of the season. They break into the win

Interleague play began against Milwaukee. The Cubs and White Sox then met in old-time uniforms (below).

The scoring output ties the modern franchise record, established in 1922. **Luis Gonzalez** homers and drives in six runs, and Sosa goes 4-for-6 with a home run and four RBIs. **Scott Bullett** comes off the bench for two late-game at-bats—and contributes a double and triple and four RBIs. ... On September 25 at Wrigley Field, Cubs righthander **Frank Castillo** loses his no-hit bid with two out in the ninth inning when St. Louis' **Bernard Gilkey** hits a triple on a 2-2 pitch.

Castillo finishes with a one-hitter and 13 strike-outs in a 7-0 triumph. ... Castillo's masterpiece comes in an eight-game Cubs winning streak that pushes the team over .500. ... Sosa reaches 100 RBIs for the first time, finishing with 119. He hits 36 homers. ... Grace finishes fifth in the N.L. batting race at .326. ... Myers records 38 saves. ... The Cubs' 73-71 record is good for third place. ... On October 31, Sandberg announces he will return as a player in 1996 after the absence of a season

CHICAGO **CUBS** V S **MILWAUKEE BREWERS**

Battle of the Border
June 13, 1997
LINCOLN NAVIGATOR

column with a 4-3 victory in the second game of an April 20 doubleheader against the Mets in New York. ... After their 0-14 start, the Cubs go 43-44 before enduring a nine-game losing streak. ... Interleague play begins in the majors. In their first regular-season game against an A.L. team, the Cubs lose to the Milwaukee Brewers, 4-2, on June 13. Three days later, the Cubs take on the White Sox in the clubs' first official meeting since the 1906 World Series. Righthander **Kevin Foster** beats the Sox, 8-3. ... The Cubs finish at 68-94 and in last place. ... In his final year, Sandberg hits 12 home runs and finishes with 282 over 16 seasons. His career total as a second baseman, 277, is a major league

record. ... Sosa has 36 homers and 119 RBIs. ... The Cubs' leader in wins, **Jeremi Gonzalez**, posts only 11 victories.

1998

The expansion Arizona Diamondbacks (N.L.) and Tampa Bay Devil Rays (A.L.) begin play, and the N.L. Central grows to six teams as the Brewers leave the American League and join the division. ... Making only his fifth major league start, righthander **Kerry Wood** sets a National League record with a 20-strikeout game against Houston on May 6. He allows only one hit. ... The **Mark McGwire**-**Sammy Sosa** home run race grips the nation. The Cardinals' McGwire wins out, 70-66, as **Roger Maris'** single-season record of 61 falls. ... Sitting on the record for most home runs (246) at the start of a career without a grand slam, Sosa hits a bases-loaded shot at Arizona on July 27. He hits another grand slam the next night. ... Wood misses the last month of the regular season because of an elbow injury. ... The Cubs overcome a wrenching loss in Milwaukee on September 23 and qualify for post-season play. In the game at County Stadium, Chicago leads, 7-5, in the ninth inning when Cubs defensive replacement **Brant Brown** drops a two-out, bases-loaded fly ball—a muff that clears the bases and gives the Brewers an 8-7 victory. ...

Mark McGwire got the best of Sosa in their riveting 1998 homer battle, but Sosa received 438 MVP votes compared with runner-up Big Mac's total of 272.

Gary Gaetti

2000

Don Baylor takes over as manager. ... The Cubs and Mets open the N.L. season in Tokyo, splitting two games. ... Wood returns to the Cubs in May and goes on to post an 8-7 record. His return isn't enough to overcome the team's dismal perform- ance. Chicago is 35-51 at the All-Star Game break and, after a 14-4 spurt, fin- ishes the season with a 16-42 thud. ... Sosa wins his first home run crown. He hits .320 in his 50- homer, 138-RBI season. ... Second baseman **Eric Young** steals 54 bases. ... Only righthander **Jon Lieber** (12-11) wins more than eight games for the 65-97 Cubs, who again finish sixth.

After Chicago and San Francisco finish the regu- lar season tied for the wild-card spot at 89-73, the Cubs win a September 28 playoff game against the Giants, 5-3, at Wrigley Field as **Gary Gaetti** hits a two- run homer and **Matt Mieske** contributes a two-run pinch single. ... In N.L. Division Series play, the Braves sweep the Cubs in three games. Wood returns to action when he starts against Atlanta in Game 3 and allows only one run and three hits over five innings. ... Sosa, who drives in an N.L.-high 158 runs, is voted the league's MVP. ... Wood, who goes 13-6, is the N.L. Rookie of the Year. ...Righthander **Kevin**

Tapani wins 19 games. ... **Rod Beck** amasses 51 saves.

1999

Wood makes one spring-training start–and is shut down three days later when tests show a complete ligament tear in his elbow. He misses the entire season. ... After a 32-23 start, the Cubs lose 50 of their next 70 games. They plummet from post- season participants to last-place finishers (67- 95). ... The pitching staff's 5.27 ERA ranks next to last in the N.L. The team's .257 batting mark also is one notch from the bot- tom. ... Sosa has a ringing encore to his magical sea- son of '98, blasting 63

homers (two fewer than McGwire). ... Grace (.309) hits above .300 for the fifth consecutive season and the seventh time in eight years.

2001

The Cubs get off to a 20-11 start. ... Third base- man **Bill Mueller** frac- tures a kneecap on May

Don Baylor

The Cubs began the 2000 season far away from home, splitting two games in Tokyo.

13 and is out for three months. ... After an eight-game losing streak in May drops the surprising Cubs out of first place, Baylor's team wins 12 in a row and 20 out of 25 to surge back on top. Chicago stays there until mid-August. ... Needing another big bat in their lineup to help Sosa, the Cubs carry on a nearly three-week dalliance with Tampa Bay slugger **Fred McGriff** before the Devil Rays' first baseman agrees to waive a no-trade contract. The deal is made July 27, a day on which the Cubs have a four-game lead in the N.L. Central. ... Tendinitis forces Wood onto the disabled list on

Eric Young

Fred McGriff

August 4. He misses five weeks, during which the Cubs tumble from atop the standings to 4½ games out of first place. ... The Cubs slip to third by season's end (88-74, five games behind both the Astros and Cardinals). ... Sosa hits 64 home runs and drives in a league-leading 160 runs. ... McGriff contributes 12 homers and 41 RBIs in 49 games. ... Lieber is a 20-game winner. ... Wood is 12-6.

2002

Heralded Cubs prospect **Mark Prior**, after six starts in Class AA and three in Class AAA, makes his major league debut on May 22 at Wrigley Field. In a winning effort, he strikes out 10 Pittsburgh hitters over six innings and allows four hits and two runs. ... Baylor is fired as manager on July 5. The Cubs' record is 34-49. **Bruce Kimm**, manager at Class AAA Iowa, is named Baylor's successor. ... Sosa sets an N.L. record with a total of 14 RBIs in two consecutive games. On August 10 at Colorado, he hits three-run homers in the third, fourth and fifth innings; the next day, he hammers a grand slam and an RBI double against the Rockies. His nine-RBI game ties the club record set by Heinie Zimmerman in 1911. ... On August 29 at Milwaukee, the Cubs' **Mark Bellhorn** becomes the first player in N.L. history to homer from both

Mark Bellhorn

sides of the plate in one inning. Batting righthanded, he hits a two-run shot off **Andrew Lorraine** in the fourth inning; later in the 10-run inning, he bats lefthanded and slugs a three-run blast off **Jose Cabrera**. ... Sosa tops the league in homers with 49. McGriff hits 30 and Bellhorn 27. ... Wood and **Matt Clement** are 12-11. Prior is 6-6. ... The Cubs finish fifth at 67-95.

2003

Dusty Baker, who had led the Giants to the World Series in 2002, takes over as Cubs manager. ... Sosa hits the 500th home run of his major league career, connecting against the Reds' **Scott Sullivan** on April 4 in Cincinnati. ... Sosa is ejected from a June 3 game against Tampa Bay when cork is found in his

shattered bat, and draws an eight-game suspension. After Sosa's appeal, the suspension (which begins June 11) is reduced by one game. ... The Yankees' **Roger Clemens** goes for his 300th career victory in a June 7 game against Chicago at Wrigley Field. He loses, 5-2, to Wood and the Cubs when **Eric Karros** hits reliever **Juan Acevedo**'s first pitch for a three-run homer in the seventh inning. ... On June 26, Prior strikes out 16 Milwaukee batters in eight innings but the Cubs lose when **Joe Borowski**, who relieves Prior to begin the ninth, yields a three-run homer to **Geoff Jenkins**. ... Center fielder **Corey Patterson**, hitting .298 with 13 homers and 55 RBIs in 83 games, is lost for the season when he suffers a knee injury on July 6 against St. Louis. ...

At the All-Star Game break, Baker's team is in third place with a 47-47 record. ... In three trades made over a four-week period beginning July 22, the Cubs obtain center fielder **Kenny Lofton**, third baseman **Aramis Ramirez** and first baseman **Randall Simon** from the Pirates and second baseman **Tony Womack** from the Rockies. ... On August 22 at Arizona, Sosa slams

Eric Karros

Kenny Lofton

two homers off **Curt Schilling**—the second his 500th as a Cub. Chicago wins, 4-1, as **Carlos Zambrano** pitches no-hit ball for 7⅔ innings. ... The Cubs win four of five games against St. Louis in early September at Wrigley. The fiercely contested series, which features an 8-7 Cubs victory in a game in which Chicago trailed 6-0, lifts Baker's team past the Cardinals and into second place—just a half-game behind first-place

Houston. ... Entering the final weekend, the Astros and Cubs are tied for the N.L. Central lead. Houston loses Friday night and Saturday against Milwaukee and the Cubs, rained out on Friday, sweep a doubleheader from Pittsburgh on Saturday to take the division crown. ... Chicago finishes with an 88-74 record. ... The Cubs win a postseason series for the first time since 1908 by defeating the Braves in five games in the Division

Series. ... After leading the NLCS three games to one and then being five outs away in Game 6 from their first World Series appearance in 58 years, the Cubs wind up losing to Florida in seven games. A fan's interference with a catchable Marlins foul ball in the eighth inning of Game 6 becomes a part of Cubs lore—and angst. ... Ron Santo's No. 10 is retired. Santo joins Ernie Banks (14) and Billy Williams (26) as the only Cubs so honored.

2004

After the club acquires first baseman **Derrek Lee** in an offseason trade with Florida and signs former Cubs pitching star Maddux to a free-agent contract, expectations are

high. ... The Cubs are dealt a huge setback in the spring: Prior has Achilles' tendon and elbow problems. He misses the first two months of the season. ... Seven weeks into Prior's time on the disabled list, Wood goes down with a triceps injury and doesn't pitch for two months. ... In mid-May, Sosa injures his back while sneezing and is sidelined for a month. ... A rotator-cuff tear ends closer Borowski's season in early June. Borowski had saved 33 games in 2003. ... The Cubs bend but don't break—they are 47-40 at the All-Star break, seven games behind the N.L. Central-leading Cardinals. ... In a four-way trade July 31, the Cubs acquire star Red Sox shortstop **Nomar**

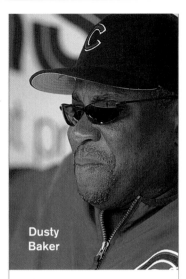

Dusty Baker

Garciaparra. ... Maddux wins the 300th game of his major league career at San Francisco on August 7. He works into the sixth inning of an 8-4 victory. ... Though Prior, Wood and Sosa return to reasonably good health, none shows his '03 form—yet the

Cubs, making good use of the long ball, put together 11-4 and 8-1 spurts in July and August. They then mount a 13-3 run in September, go a season-high 21 games over .500 and, with St. Louis running away with the division title, have a wild-card postseason berth in their sights. ... Having gone 8-2 in the first 10 games of their last road trip of the season and built a wild-card lead of 1½ games, Chicago takes a 3-0 lead into the bottom of the ninth inning of a September 25 game at New York. Closer **LaTroy Hawkins** yields a two-out, two-strike, three-run home run to the Mets' **Victor Diaz**. In the 11th, **Craig Brazell**'s homer off **Kent Mercker** wins it for the New Yorkers. The

Derrek Lee

Nomar Garciaparra

Caray and Stone depart in the offseason. They are replaced by **Len Kasper**, TV voice of the Florida Marlins, and **Bob Brenly**, former Diamondbacks manager. ... Garciaparra signs a one-year contract with the Cubs.

2005

Ryne Sandberg is elected to the Baseball Hall of Fame in early January. Needing 387 votes for induction, Sandberg is named on 393 ballots. He accompanies **Wade Boggs** into the Cooperstown shrine. ... Rumors about a possible Sosa trade heat up. Suitors include the Mets and Orioles. ... In late January, an agreement is reached (with details still to be worked out) to send Sosa to Baltimore.

Cubs lose again the next day at Shea Stadium. ... After starting the ensuing final homestand with a victory over Cincinnati, the Cubs drop three in a row to the Reds—including consecutive 12-inning games, one in which Hawkins again is one strike away from nailing down a victory, the other wasting 16 strikeouts by Prior in nine innings—and then lose two straight to the Braves. The seven-losses-in-eight-games skid eliminates Baker's team from postseason contention. ... Sosa leaves early on the final day of the season, incurring the wrath of the team and the front office (which fines him $87,400 for his disappearing act). Earlier in the season, Sosa had been unhappy over being dropped in the batting order. He also thought he was being blamed for the Cubs' disappointing year. ... The Cubs set a franchise record with 235 homers, with Alou hitting 39, Ramirez 36, Sosa 35 and Lee 32. ... Ramirez has two three-homer games. ... Sosa's first-inning home run on April 18 against the Reds is his 513th as a Cub, breaking Banks' franchise record. He finishes the year with 574 homers overall, seventh on the majors' all-time list. ... Garciaparra, hampered by injuries, hits .297 in 43 games. ... Zambrano winds up 16-8 and Maddux 16-11 for the 89-73 Cubs, who finish one game better than in 2003 but slip to third place. ... The club posts consecutive winning seasons for the first time since 1971 and 1972. ... Wrigley Field attendance tops 3 million for the first time. ... Cubs relievers blow 24 save opportunities, and the team is 19-30 in one-run games. ... Spats with umpires, the media and television analyst **Steve Stone** make for a contentious year. ... TV play-by-play man **Chip**

Ryne Sandberg